CONVICT SYDNEY

The real-life stories of 32 prisoners.

Jennifer Twemlow

Copyright © 2020 Jennifer Twemlow

Publishing Services by Happy Self Publishing
www.happyselfpublishing.com

Year: 2020

All rights reserved. No reproduction, transmission or copy of this publication can be made without the written consent of the author in accordance with the provision of the Copyright Acts. Any person doing so will be liable to civil claims and criminal prosecution.

Happy Self Publishing.

Contents

Introduction 1

James Milward..5

Tom Tough 14

Elizabeth Sullivan 22

Ann Armsden 28

Frederick Mitton...39

John Dwyer 46

James Frazer 52

Robert Hudson 57

George Vigers 64

Alexander Green 71

Mary Morgan..79

Israel Chapman 88

Ann Yates 93

Catherine Edwards 99

Ann Birmingham 104

Stephen Little 111

Charles Anderson 116

Mary Jackman 120

William Henshall 125

Robert Sidaway 128

Ann Jarvis 133

William Cluer 138

Samuel Wheeler 143

Abraham Lawley 148

Ann Moran 155

John Lane 157

William Lock Thurston 160

John McEntire 166

Francis Ambrose 172

Catherine Harvey 176

Frederick Brook Carrick 184

Isaac Crane 192

Glossary 198

Bibliography 202

Acknowledgements 256

Introduction

The Industrial Revolution created mass unemployment in Great Britain and Ireland. Out of work farmers flocked to the major cities in search of work. Faced with the inability to provide food for their families many were forced into a life of crime. During this time the courts sent alarming numbers of people to prison for minor offences. Britain began sending its convicted felons to America to relieve the pressure on their prisons, but when the American War of Independence ended in 1783 that was no longer an option.

A temporary solution to this growing problem was to house them in hulks. Moored retired ships were converted into floating prisons and could be seen dotted along the river Thames and in other major cities. During the day convicts spent ten to twelve hours performing hard labour on government projects throughout the city and at night they slept in the hulks. It wasn't long until these too were heaving with prisoners and, consequently, diseases such as typhoid and cholera became rife. Another solution was desperately needed.

Australia had been on Britain's radar since Captain Cook discovered it in 1770 and returned with glowing accounts of its flora and fauna. Sending convicts to Australia ticked a lot of boxes. It enabled easy access to whaling grounds and China's trading routes, while providing a military outpost on the other side of the world. It was also a strategic move to prevent countries such as France creating a presence there.

In 1788 the First Fleet sailed into Botany Bay, the site recommended by Cook. There were eleven ships in total – three were filled with supplies and livestock, two were naval vessels and the remaining six were filled with convicts. Due to its poor soil quality, its unprotected harbour and its insufficient supply of fresh water, Botany Bay was abandoned. Days later the weary convoy sailed into Port Jackson after Captain Phillip declared Sydney Cove a suitable location and disembarked. The area was already known fondly as Warrane by the Gadigal people. The arrival forced them from their land and denied them of their natural resources.

Over the next eighty years, roughly 166,000 convict men, women and children were sent out to Australia. According to Ancestry.com the average age of the convicts was twenty-two, the most common sentence was seven years, with petty theft being the most common crime. The records also reveal an astonishing imbalance of the sexes – about one woman to every six men.

This book is a collection of randomly selected convicts who were sent to Sydney during this period. It's not a compilation of the most successful or the worst offenders, but a medley of the everyday citizens who lived and breathed in Sydney town. Each character has been brought to life with glimpses into their personalities and their social lives. Their individual experiences offer a broader insight into the daily happenings of Sydney and the convict system.

We step inside early Sydney as it was taking shape and come to understand the types of work, routines, punishments, rewards, uniforms, marriage restrictions and so much more by walking in a convict's shoes. *Convict Sydney* also explores what life was like after convicts had completed their sentences, how they eked out a living and created their new identities in their tight-knit but ever growing community. This is an opportunity to immerse ourselves in the lives of some of the people that shaped our nation.

James Milward

Ship: Layton
Approximate age on arrival: 16 years old
Crime: Shop robbery
Sentence: Death commuted to 14 years
Date arrived: 8 November 1829

James Milward was a wayward sixteen year old boy from Derby who was caught stealing and sentenced to fourteen years transportation. He was 5 foot 6 inches tall with brown hair and hazel eyes and had a nose that leaned to the right. In March 1829 he walked into the grocery shop that belonged to a man named Mr Glass and asked for some oil. When the man who served him went to fetch the oil, James's accomplice William snuck in and stole the till. When the unsuspecting man returned and saw it missing he seized James and called the police.

At the time of the robbery, James had been working at a Mr Towle's mill along with William who worked as a tailor. They both resided at Borrowash, a small village in Derbyshire. This was not the first time they had robbed a shop. Only a few days earlier they stole some cheese from a place in Ockbrook. When their case was heard the judge handed them both, the death sentence, which was later commuted to fourteen years transportation.

Shortly after being sentenced James was deported. He spent close to five months at sea travelling to New South Wales. James was one of 190 convict men kept below deck. The conditions were cramped, the ceiling was low and it was damp and painfully hot. They were starved of natural light and fresh air. Besides the sounds coming from the other men, James would have heard the water rushing past the hull and the creaking and groaning of the ship as the wood flexed. The ropes would be singing as they strained to the pressure of the sails taut against the wind, stretching them to near breaking point. He could hear the sailors spurred into action — bounding across the deck above his head, as they answered to the ship's bell, which was rung every half hour around the clock, using their whistles to communicate with each other over the roar of the ocean.

As the journey progressed, the noxious smell of so many sweaty, unwashed men living in close proximity intensified. Their clothing was now threadbare, their teeth rotting and their skin caked in filth. Despite living in conditions ripe for the breeding of diseases, there were surprisingly only two deaths during the journey.

On the 8th November 1829 the *Layton* sailed into Port Jackson. It was a windy, rainy day, but relatively warm at 23 degrees. The convicts confined below deck would have been itching to set their feet on solid ground, but it would be nine long days before they would be let off the ship. Before that could happen, the necessary administration had to be performed. Officials came on board and inspected the ship, passengers and cargo. Reports were made about the trip, the state of the convicts and any deaths, injuries and illnesses that had occurred.

On the third day James and his fellow convicts were brought up on deck for muster. Their senses were assaulted with the blinding sunshine and the smell of fresh sea air that whipped around them, stirring up the foul odour emanating from their bodies. It was then that they got their first glimpse of this strange new land that was so very different from home. As they took it in and tried to imagine what lay ahead they were told to strip to their waist while their indents were written up. A clerk went from convict to convict, recording every detail about them, from their height, weight, crime to a description of their tattoos and any scars they might have had. They were also asked what skills they had so they could be appropriately assigned.

On disembarking James was assigned to Mr Raffly at Castle Hill, however this was short-lived as he absconded. As punishment, he was sent to Cockatoo Island, a dumping ground for repeat offenders. Convicts on the island were given the back-breaking job of quarrying stone for the various public works commissioned at the time such as building granary silos, official residences and the Fitzroy Dock. Life on the island was extremely brutal and escape was near impossible as the island was surrounded by shark-infested waters. Only one man is recorded as having escaped, by swimming to Balmain in 1863. His name was Frederick Ward, better known as Captain Thunderbolt, and once ashore he absconded into the bush with the aid of his Aboriginal wife.

In 1836, through good behaviour, James earned himself a Ticket of Leave making him a 'Ticketer'. Tickets of Leave allowed a convict to find their own accommodation and employment within a confined district. It was a piece of paper that they had to carry on them at all times. If found without it, they were treated as runaways and locked up. It could mean the loss of their privileges. It was a great system for the government too, as it took convicts off the 'King's stores' and relieved the growing problem of housing.

However, James soon lost his Ticket of Leave for stealing fowls. His bad behaviour continued, earning him fourteen days in solitary confinement and three years added to his sentence for yet another robbery. He served the rest of his sentence out in Hyde Park Barracks which was built in 1819 to house convicts.

Hyde Park Barracks is a three storey Georgian building designed by the convict architect Francis Greenway and was built by convicts. It was built to relieve the problems in the community of convicts trying to find their own accommodation, staying out late getting drunk and disorderly and committing further crimes. For years convicts worked from sunrise till 3 o'clock in the afternoon. When they knocked off for the day they were allowed to work for themselves in order to save money to find lodgings, but many found themselves homeless and living in the streets. Building the Barracks allowed the government to have more control of their movements and work them till sunset.

The Barracks had a high wall surrounding it. Within the courtyard, the northern side had privies, a bakehouse, watchhouses, solitary confinement cells, storage rooms, and the residence and office of the superintendent. On the southern side, there was a kitchen with long mess rooms. The courtyard was used for musters and floggings. It was designed to house 600 convicts, but more than double that were crammed in. Unlike other government housing, it was a classless system.

Convicts living in the Barracks followed a strict routine. They woke at dawn, worked till lunchtime, and had an hour for lunch before returning to work until sunset. The evenings were spent playing cards or making cabbage tree hats to trade or sell. On Sundays, they would shave and dress in their best and were marched across the road to St James church to enjoy the service.

Overall, for most convicts, the Barracks was a luxury. Many had come from living on the streets, not knowing when their next feed would be. At the Barracks they had a roof over their head, clothes on their back and the promise of regular meals. Their rations were minimal, and they were given the same thing day in and day out. For breakfast, they ate hominy or gruel. They were only given one other meal per day - a stew with meat and vegetables grown by the convicts in the kitchen gardens, more often than not cabbage, potatoes and onions. They could mop up their stew with bread that was baked in the bakehouse onsite and wash it down with tea. Salt and sugar were also distributed to make their black tea and bland meals more palatable.

The Hyde Park Barracks is still standing today and is a living museum. Visitors can hear the crunch of red gravel under their feet as they cross the courtyard, run their hands along the lime-washed walls, look up to the spectacular roof and contemplate the life of a convict whilst lying in a hammock.

By 1845, the number of convicts living at the Barracks was dwindling as transportation to Australia was coming to an end. James was right at the end of his sentence and would have been contemplating life as a free man. One Saturday night at the end of May at roughly 7 pm, James was making a cabbage tree hat when he got into a silly argument with a fellow convict named Edgerton. The two had always got along, but fell into a disagreement over the hat stick. The argument deteriorated into a shoving match. During the scuffle, a bucket of liquid - probably a bucket which serviced them as a toilet by night - was knocked over. Edgerton pushed James who slipped on the liquid which sent him flying backwards. On the way down he hit his head quite severely against a hammock beam which rendered him unconscious. Edgerton was distraught and immediately regretful for his actions. He assisted James until he was taken to the hospital next door.

Unfortunately, James didn't make it. When examining him, Doctor Silver found that James had a diseased blood vessel at the base of his brain. The fall and knock on the head had ruptured the blood vessel which would otherwise not have killed him. Edgerton faced a jury at the Three Tons Tavern but they came back with the verdict of 'accidental homicide'.

Tom Tough

Ship: Marquis of Hastings (4)
Approximate age on arrival: 30 years old
Crime: Robbery
Sentence: Life
Date arrived: 23 July 1839

At 5 foot 4 inches tall with black woolly hair, a broad flat nose and piercing black eyes, Tom Tough would have been a striking, formidable figure as he stepped off the ship at Sydney Cove. He was one of the few 'men of colour' to be transported to the colonies. His face was covered in scars and he was missing a front tooth which was most likely a sign of a tribal rite of passage.

Tom was originally from Antigua, Britain's 'Gateway to the Caribbean', and was a descendant of the former African slave trade. At the time of his arrest Tom was living in Antigua with his wife and two children and working as a pastry cook. On 1 April 1834, Tom was tried and convicted of robbery and sentenced to life. He was later sent to England and in 1838 he waited in incarceration on board the prison hulk *York* which was moored in Gosport before being transported to Van Diemen's Land (now known as Tasmania) and then on to Sydney.

Tom was continually getting into trouble. He was transferred to Newcastle as punishment but then he reoffended and was sent back to Sydney. It wasn't until he was sentenced to go to Cockatoo Island that he started to worry. Cockatoo Island had a bad reputation and he wasn't looking forward to going there. Tom was transferred to the Hyde Park Barracks and was locked up in the watchhouse along with other offending convicts to await his passage.

On Thursday 29 January 1842, just before midnight, his fellow inmates called to the guard for water. When the unsuspecting guard opened the cell door a group of convicts rushed him, knocked him down, and made a run for it. Tom immediately sounded the alarm and pinned one of the men down to prevent him from escaping. A few did manage to scale the high Barracks wall, but most were captured, thanks to Tom. A recommendation was made to the Governor that Tom's sentence be changed. He was granted a reprieve from Cockatoo Island and taken out of the cells to begin work with the yard men. Tom was elated and promised 'never more to be in de chokey for bad conduct'.

The government tried to provide incentive for good behaviour by offering rewards. Rewards came in many forms, such as extra rations, tobacco and favourable treatment. A convict might be given free time outside the Barracks after work and allowed to work for oneself during that time if they chose. Married men with families living back home could apply to have their wives and children sent out. Married men could also live in their own private lodgings with their families. The Ticket of Leave and Pardons were highly sought after rewards. Another reward was being given positions of trust such as Police Officers, Gatekeepers and Messengers.

Tom must have been inspired by his reward as he kept up the good behaviour and two years later he was granted a Ticket of Leave. This Ticket allowed him to remain and work in the district of Windsor. Shortly after, Tom met and fell in love with another convict named Priscilla Marshall. Priscilla was originally from Jamaica and was a year older than Tom. Like Tom, she had been sentenced for life, and had arrived on the *Elizabeth*. In 1844 Tom made an application to marry Priscilla.

All convicts had to apply for marriage and they were usually successful. The government encouraged marriage as it brought a sense of morality to the community. They also used the incentive of free land to encourage convicts to marry, with additional free land granted for each child that resulted from the union. Unfortunately, Tom and Priscilla's request was denied as he was still legally married to someone in Antigua. But Tom was determined to make Priscilla his bride and continued making requests for marriage. Finally, three years later he and Priscilla were granted approval. They married in Windsor on the 19 May 1847.

A year into their marriage Tom was granted a Conditional Pardon which meant he was a free citizen. His Pardon forbade him to go to Great Britain, Ireland or back to his homeland in Antigua. It would be another five years before Priscilla earned hers. Tom and Priscilla marked their freedom by choosing and using the new surname Webster. Former convicts often changed their name or spelt their surname slightly differently to hide from their criminal past and start a new life. During this period the couple welcomed the birth of their only child.

In 1853 Tom began to work as a cook again for the Kings Arms situated in Pitt Street. However, he wasn't there long as he was mistreated by the owner, who accused him of stealing. Mrs Stone described him to the court as having '… an ogre's face, and an equally matched black wife.' She also asserted that Priscilla was attending to the 'comforts of wayfarers'. Tom was called to the stand and told the court of his mistreatment at the hands of Mrs Stone. He claimed that she had not paid him for his week's work and had 'cum in de kitchen, 'buse me, call me black brute, cannibal'. Tom was 'struck dumb' when the judge ruled in his favour and dismissed the charges against him.

A month later, Priscilla left Tom. Devastated, Tom put several advertisements in the paper pleading for his wife to come back to him and their child. He warned others not to harbour his runaway wife. He also stated that he would not pay for any expenses that she incurred. He searched for her for a year, but it came to nothing. He eventually accepted that she wasn't coming back and tried to move on. Sometime later he started up a relationship with another coloured woman named Sophia Henry.

Tom and Sophia's relationship blossomed quickly. It wasn't long before Sophia moved into Tom's place in May's Lane off Parramatta Street. On the morning of 25 September 1854 Tom went to the local jewellery store in Hunter Street to purchase a ring for Sophia. He was served by the owner's wife Mrs Julia Hughes. Mrs Hughes showed Tom several rings from a box in the window and after much deliberation and further browsing around the store Tom settled on one that was priced at 40 shillings. He paid a 10 shilling deposit and asked Mrs Hughes to have the ring engraved with some initials. Tom then left the store but returned at lunchtime and again that evening. By this time Mrs Hughes was beginning to get suspicious and, when not otherwise engaged with customers, she kept an eye on Tom.

The following morning Mrs Hughes' daughter, Isabella, was doing her daily dusting of the window displays when she noticed a box containing 100 gold rings was missing. The police were summoned and Mrs Hughes told them that she suspected Tom was behind the theft. The police confronted Tom and Sophia at their home in May's Lane. As Tom was denying any involvement Sophia tried to slip a ring off her finger unnoticed. However, the police officer did notice and grabbed her hand, forcing her to relinquish the said ring. Tom quickly explained that he had found the ring on George Street. The police officer took Tom and Sophia into custody and took the ring in as evidence. Mrs Hughes later identified the ring as one belonging to her husband.

On Thursday 16 November 1854 Tom and Sophia were brought to trial. The jury acquitted Sophia but Tom was charged with larceny and sentenced to 12 months labour in Sydney Gaol. The box of jewellery was never found. It's unknown what became of his child to Priscilla.

After serving his time he was arrested again for stealing pictures and earned himself fourteen more days labour. The last mention of him was in 1867, he would have been roughly 58 years old and, sadly, he was homeless and living on the streets of Sydney. The police picked him up and he was charged with vagrancy and sent to Tarban Creek Lunatic Asylum.

Elizabeth Sullivan

Ship: Elizabeth (5)
Approximate age on arrival: 19 years old
Crime: Stealing clothes
Sentence: 7 years
Date arrived: 12 October 1836

Elizabeth Sullivan was sent to the colony for stealing clothing, arriving when she was just nineteen years of age. She had been living in London with a man named Thomas Charles Dixon. The couple were renting the upstairs room in a home about 150 yards from a public house. One night they went there for a drink and to play a few games of bagatelle, which is very similar to billiards.

The bar was relatively quiet that particular night. Benjamin Whitcombe, a trader in earthenware and other goods, had joined the couple. He had brought with him a bundle of items – 8 pairs of stockings, 2 handkerchiefs, 6 pairs of braces, a pair of gloves and 2 bells. When Elizabeth and Thomas had left for the night, Mr Whitcombe got up to leave and discovered the bundle missing. The police were notified and they immediately went to the couple's lodgings where they discovered the bundle on the lawn. It was believed that they threw the bundle out the window when they realised the police were coming for them.

Their trial was heard at The Old Bailey in London on 29 February 1836 and, although they both denied any involvement, the couple were both sentenced to seven years transportation. Thomas was put on the ship called *Moffat*, Elizabeth was on the *Elizabeth 5*. Although destined for the same shores, they did not reunite in any romantic way, although they undoubtedly would have crossed paths with Sydney being such a small town.

Elizabeth arrived in 1836 and soon became one of the most colourful characters in Sydney. She was known as the 'Fighting Hen of Cooks

River', and would take on any woman in the ring. She ruled the Cooks River area with her fighting skills, her flamboyant style of dress and her heavily tattooed arms. She had no tolerance for bad manners or foul language. She had a reputation for being tough, pugnacious and intimidated people with her confidence. One newspaper described her as a 'tall, powerful woman' with 'buffalo-like dimensions'.

Elizabeth was to meet her match a few years later with Joseph Hilton, a fellow convict. Joseph arrived on *Hercules 2*. He was 5ft 6 inches tall with brown hair and hazel eyes. He had come from Southhampton, England where he'd worked as a labourer. In 1840 Joseph applied to the government for permission to make Elizabeth his wife. The application was granted and soon after they were married. The couple set up a home in Cooks River near Botany Bay and soon became well known amongst the local residents. Her husband was known about town as 'Joe the Basket Maker' and was regularly in the press, daring any man, woman, dog or cock to take him and his household on in the ring.

The couple never backed down from a fight whether it was in the ring or in the courtroom.

Elizabeth was in court several times claiming to be a victim of foul language and assault. Her attire was so flamboyant that newspapers spent more time describing her appearance than the actual court cases. She wore colourful gowns with the latest patterns and satin bonnets which were elaborately decorated with a variety of flowers and fruits. Her appearance may have been contrived to remind the court that although she was known as the 'Fighting Hen of Cooks River', she was still a lady and deserved to be treated as one.

Convict uniforms stripped them of their identity, so it was not uncommon for former convicts to splash out on fine clothes when their sentence was over and they had earned some real money. Clothing such as the magpie, a yellow and black punishment suit, was designed to humiliate the wearer as well as keep them visible. So too was shaving women's heads, as it robbed a woman of her femininity. Their clothing was stamped with a broad arrow, marking them as another piece of government property.

Dressing well blurred the lines of class and gave them a sense of individuality. Although people tried to emulate British society with their dress sense and copied the new styles coming out of Europe, a new attitude towards fashion was beginning in the colony. People of all classes were forgetting about the rules dictated by their class. The upper classes were finding that they had to work and get dirty and chose more comfortable, practical attire, particularly in rural areas. People chose to dress up for special events such as picnics, the races, the theatre, etc. They also adapted their clothing to the hot climate by choosing fabrics such as cotton that breathed and made cabbage tree hats to protect themselves from the sun.

Elizabeth knew how to use fashion to her advantage. Walking into a courtroom with flashy clothing made people forget that she was a former criminal and instead look at her as a lady with money who was worthy of respect.

In 1841 Joe was granted an Absolute Pardon and Elizabeth received her Certificate of Freedom two years later. An Absolute Pardon and a Certificate of Freedom were very similar – they both gave convicts their freedom and allowed them to travel back to the United Kingdom if they pleased. Absolute Pardons were only issued to convicts with a life sentence and the Certificate of Freedom was issued to convicts who had completed their sentences.

Ann Armsden

Ship: Lady Juliana
Approximate age on arrival: 26 years old
Crime: Highway Robbery
Sentence: Death commuted to 7 years
Date arrived: 6 June 1790

It was the beginning of Spring in the year 1787 when Ann and her friends Jonathan Williams and Ann Fortescue robbed a lady in Deptford, Kent. There were two parts of Deptford – St Nicholas and St Paul. It was on the Kings Highway in St Paul's parish where they attacked a woman named Mary Brown, robbing her of her harrateen, a fabric used for curtains and bedding, some stockings and her husband's linen shirt and breeches. Mary claimed to be in fear of her life. Jonathan was found not guilty, but the two girls were sentenced to be hanged. Both their sentences were later commuted to either 7 or 14 years (the records vary) and they were imprisoned awaiting transportation. Ann was single and only 23 years of age at the time of her incarceration. Her friend was about 27 years old. They both endured prison life for a couple of years before they were put on a ship bound for New Holland.

The girls arrived in Port Jackson on the infamous *Lady Juliana,* otherwise known as the 'floating brothel'. The convicts on board were made up of over 200 females, mostly London prostitutes, thieves and the like. The instant the ship left the docks the men on board had their pick of the women passengers, many making them their wives. This was common practice out at sea and at the time a newspaper reported the practice as 'law'. With all the sexual activity on board, it is a wonder that so few women fell pregnant. Although contraceptive devices weren't completely unheard of, they were rare. The experienced women must have had their own methods.

The *Lady Juliana's* voyage to New South Wales took longer than any other convict ship. It made stops along the way at Tenerife and St Jago, islands off West Africa, and at the very tip of South Africa at the Cape of Good Hope. They also spent about forty-five days in Rio De Janeiro, Brazil. Each stop was an opportunity to restock the ship with fresh food and water. The decks were scrubbed clean and overall the women were treated very well by the officers. The time at each stop was often spent in debauchery, with the women entertaining the men's carnal appetites and satisfying their licentious needs. The officers turned a blind eye.

Back on board, below deck, gangs were formed and one of the leaders called Nance was subjected to a humiliating punishment after breaking into the bulkhead where the alcohol was stored and holding a drinking party for herself and her crew. Later, above deck, she went from one officer to another, swearing like a true sailor, and climbed the quarterdeck, an act that even an officer would have been flogged for. Nance was seized and a barrel was fashioned with holes for arms and placed over her like a dress. At first she made a big joke of it, strutting her stuff down the ship, dancing and smoking a cigar. However, after a few hours, the weight of the barrel began to take its toll and she begged to be let out of it.

Cramming so many people below deck in such a confined space had its challenges, but even more so for women. As time went by their menstrual cycles would have no doubt synchronized. During the day the women used toilets above deck at the head of the ship. But by night, locked three levels below the main deck, in the dark, damp orlop, they would have shared buckets. The stench permeating from the buckets would have been overwhelming at the best of times let alone when the women were menstruating. Rats would have run rampant and the women also had to deal with the noxious smells wafting up from the bilge water in the hold below them.

The women used rags to deal with the blood flow, but with fresh water being so scarce they had the choice of washing them in sea water or keeping them to rinse out when they reached the shore. Washing them in salt water would have made them stiff and left the women very sore. For some though, the stress of being imprisoned and the whole ordeal had the effect of suppressing their menstruation. At the time, Surgeon Superintendents labelled this medical condition as 'hysteria'.

When the *Lady Juliana* finally sailed into Port Jackson, Ann and the rest of her travelling companions were met by a pitiful sight: men, women and children on the brink of starvation and in threadbare clothing. This was the first ship to arrive since the First Fleet and the surviving colony inhabitants had been desperately hoping for the ship full of supplies that they had been begging Britain for. Their looks of hope, relief and sheer joy soon turned to anger and despair when they realised it wasn't their salvation but yet more mouths to feed. The only saving grace was that it brought with it news of Britain and much yearned for letters from loved ones. About two weeks later the Second Fleet arrived with provisions just in time to save them all from certain death.

Eight weeks after disembarking the girls were separated. Ann was part of a group of 194 male and female convicts that were sent to Norfolk

Island. Her friend Ann Fortescue however, remained in Sydney and after only a few short months changed her name to Read when she married a convict named William who had come out on the *Scarborough*. She bore him two children – Sarah and Elizabeth — and then drops off the record.

Once on Norfolk Island Ann began living with a First Fleeter named George Legg. George was originally from Dorset and had been sentenced to seven years transportation for stealing a watch and other goods. He arrived on the *Charlotte* and was around the same age as Ann. A year later they were issued a sow to share with another First Fleeter named Edward Westlake. The sow produced a litter of nine piglets. It's believed they married later that year in 1791 when Reverend Richard Johnson came to the island and married a large number of convicts. The following year George got a job as night watch in Arthurs Vale and they lived on a 12 acre farm, growing wheat and breeding pigs. This was a peak time for the first settlement at Norfolk Island, with the population reaching 1156 people. And there they stayed until 1795, when they gave up their life in the country for one in the growing city of Sydney.

Ann and her husband established their home in The Rocks area of Sydney, which overlooked the harbour and had a view of any incoming ships. The harbour was the gateway to the world and the houses at The Rocks were all orientated to overlook it. The arrival of a ship could mean not only news of England but also supplies, exotic merchandise such as spices, tea and silk from China, letters from loved ones and a glimpse of the ladies disembarking with the latest fashions from Europe.

The early houses of The Rocks were crude, flimsy huts that sometimes collapsed during a heavy storm. Slowly over time, the settlers established sturdier better-built homes. By the early 1800s Ann and George were living in a weatherboard home with shingles that was fenced on all sides.

Ann and George had completed their sentences and were enjoying their freedom in this new colony with an ever-growing community. It was a chance for a new life, a new start with so many opportunities that weren't possible for them in England. However, Ann missed her family and friends, so the two scrimped and saved and bought passage on the *HMS Calcutta* in 1805 so they could go home for a visit. They had received a written grant from Governor King allowing them to leave the colony and were all set to go when the Captain of the ship revoked Ann's ticket as he didn't want women on board during wartime. Disappointed, they returned home.

Two years later in 1807 tragedy struck. On a particularly cold and windy day, George went out sailing. He was dressed in his two big thick coats. The sea was rough and George got into trouble. He was knocked overboard and his clothing made it impossible for him to save himself. Ann waited for her husband of sixteen years to come home that night but he never made it. The following morning some natives reported the incident and Ann was informed. The body was not found immediately. A hand was recovered in a shark's belly over a week later and the remainder of his body did not wash to shore for a month. Ann then had to employ some men to go and fetch it so she could give her husband a proper burial.

Ann grieved for her husband, living alone for two years. In 1809 she sold their home and the following year she met and married a local baker named George Talbot. He too was a convict, having stolen some bread from a bakery in which he worked, and had been shipped over on the *Surprise*. They built a higgledy-piggledy house with three rooms, a huge baker's oven and a deep cistern for the water needed for the bakery. The delicious smell of fresh bread that wafted from the house must have helped them attract customers.

Ann and George's stone house was unfortunately torn down around 1891 as part of the City of Sydney's improvement project. The artefacts found on the site since though, paints a picture of not the poor convict classes, but of families that had pride in their homes and themselves. There was evidence of decorative ceramics, glassware and fashionable clothing and shoes. Ann described her life with her husband in The Rocks as a 'happy and comfortable situation'.

In 1822, Ann again planned to visit Europe. She applied to the Colonial Secretary's Office for her Certificate of Freedom but was denied. She was told that they didn't have any copies of the indents for the convicts who were sent out on the *Lady Juliana* and therefore could only issue her with a Ticket of Leave. Ann had now been free for 28 years and must have been furious and extremely frustrated with the system, particularly when she knew that other women from the *Lady Juliana* had received their pardons already. She enlisted a man named John Alsop to write to the Governor Sir Thomas Brisbane on her behalf to implore him to reconsider the matter. In his letter he described her as being 'upright' with an 'irreproachable character'. The Governor's response has not survived, but there are no records of Ann on any ship lists so it's unlikely she ever fulfilled her dreams of visiting her native land.

In 1828 the couple had been married for about 18 years and were now living in Darling

Harbour. They never had any children of their own, but were providing lodgings for a convict and two children. They were also employing a labourer. However, by 1834 they were poor and infirm and moved to the Sydney Benevolent Society. On the 24 November 1835, in her early seventies, Ann died and was buried at the Elizabeth Street Burial Ground, which is where Central station stands today. Her husband George died two years later and was buried with her.

Frederick Mitton

Ship: Woodbridge
Approximate age on arrival: 30 years old
Crime: Housebreaking
Sentence: 10 years
Date arrived: 26 February 1840

Frederick arrived in the colony in February 1840 after spending only roughly four months at sea. He had left behind his wife, two sons and a daughter. Housebreaking was his first offence and he received a ten-year sentence in a courtroom in York. He was a well-educated man – he could read and write and had worked in his hometown in Lancashire as a bookkeeper. For this reason, he was not assigned to physical labour like most of the other convicts, but was given the position of watchman over the Cooks River Gang.

The Cooks River is near Botany Bay and was home to the Gadigal people. It was a small stream of fresh water which Captain Cook wrote about in his journals. It was this stream that led Captain Cook to recommend it as a site for the new colony. However, when the First Fleet arrived and gave it closer inspection it was found that the waters were too shallow for the ships and the grounds surrounding the area were swamps, so they relocated to Port Jackson.

A large gang of convicts had been sent there in 1839 to begin erecting a dam to solve Sydney's water shortage. The Tank Stream, a source of fresh water that ran through Sydney and was used by early settlers, had been abandoned in 1826 and water was being sourced from Centennial Park. This was a costly and a slow process, hence the need for a new source. Unfortunately, the new dam brought with it many environmental problems. It disrupted the ecology, it regularly flooded, and became contaminated.

The convicts of the Cooks River Gang were housed in a stockade on the north side of the river. Frederick soon became friends with three other convict men in positions of trust – Campbell an Overseer, Busby the Clerk and Storekeeper and Picken the Foreman. Campbell he already knew from the voyage over. Together they began to hatch a plan to escape the colony. It seemed like an impossible task and yet it had been done before, by Mary Bryant and her crew. But unlike the Bryants who had gone north, they planned to go south to New Zealand. They just needed provisions, a boat and a fair amount of luck.

On Friday 17 April 1840, the four men made their move. They had stolen what they needed from the government stores and had secured a cutter called the *Resolution* which was floating in the river and they set off towards the Botany Heads and out to sea. Around midnight, not long after they had left, someone noticed they were gone and alerted Mr Calvert the Superintendent. He immediately checked the stores and discovered that a large number of supplies were missing. He knew that too much had been taken for the men to carry on foot, so he raced down to the river to check the boats and discovered Mr Unwin's boat was missing from its moorings.

Calvert proceeded overland with a few of his men to Mr Goodsir's place. Goodsir was the Custom-House Officer stationed at Botany Heads. After spotting the runaway cutter the men boarded Goodsir's boat and set sail. The swell was rough but they soon caught up with the cutter and Calvert drew his loaded pistol. He ordered the men to get on board his craft and warned the offenders that if any man made the 'slightest resistance, he would blow his brains out'. The men obediently attempted to board his vessel, but the wind picked up and the swell became so big and choppy that no one was able to. After some time Calvert managed to alight the cutter followed by Goodsir. Goodsir ordered his men to take his boat back.

They tried to navigate the cutter so she could be moored safely, but the waves pushed them towards the rocks. They redirected her around the rocks, but a strong wave hit them which dashed the cutter to pieces sending everyone into the choppy sea. They swam with all their might and made it back to shore alive, except for one – Busby the Clerk and Storekeeper. He was spotted by Calvert, lying motionless between the rocks and what was left of the boat. Mitton, Campbell and Picken were locked up in the stockade and in the morning they were transported to Hyde Park Barracks to await their trial and punishment.

On 28 May 1840, the men faced their trial. Picken pleaded guilty, but Mitton and Campbell pleaded not guilty, claiming that they were only taking orders from Busby. Their defence was that Busby had enlisted them to help him transport some supplies down to Sydney. When it was Calvert's turn to state his case he informed the judge that Busby had no authority to make such a call and Mitton and Campbell knew it. All three men were sentenced to fourteen years at a penal settlement.

On 14 July 1840 Mitton was transported to Norfolk Island. Norfolk Island was re-established as a settlement in 1824 as a place to send the worst re-offending convicts. The workload and punishments were so brutal many argued that it was inhumane. Convicts were given back-breaking labour, often heavily shackled, and floggings were administered regularly and severely. When Alexander Maconochie was appointed in 1840 as Commandant of the Island the harsh treatment of convicts ceased. Luckily for Mitton, Maconochie had been appointed around the same time he arrived. Mitton kept his head down, worked hard and kept out of trouble, until eventually he was granted a Clerk position at Hyde Park Barracks.

As a clerk, Mitton saw a lot of cheques come across his desk. The temptation was too much for him and in 1847 when Mitton saw the signature of George FitzRoy, the Private Secretary of Governor-General FitzRoy, he decided it would be an easy one to forge. Mitton became friends with another convict working at the Barracks named Wilson and together they hatched a scheme. Wilson took the forged cheque and bought a coat, splitting the change with Mitton. The forgery was soon discovered and Mitton was again brought before the courts. The jury found him guilty and this time he was sentenced to three years in leg irons doing hard labour on public works.

Mitton finally learnt his lesson and in October 1850 he was granted a Ticket of Leave, enabling him to live and work in the area of Yass.

John Dwyer

Ship: Norfolk
Approximate age on arrival: 9 years old
Crime: Stealing a watch
Sentence: 7 years
Date arrived: 9 February 1832

John Dwyer was just a boy, nine years of age when he was found guilty of stealing a watch and sentenced to seven years transportation. He was taken away from his family and his home in Hampshire and spent months at sea. He was only one of a few children aboard the *Norfolk*, the rest were grown men, some hardened criminals, that he shared the dark, putrid, cramped galleys below deck with. He was a small boy of 3 foot 11 1/2 inches tall, with brown hair, grey eyes and ruddy, freckled cheeks. He had a pock-pitted face, a tell-tale sign of an earlier bout of smallpox.

When John arrived in Port Jackson he was assigned to Carters Barracks, a place for convict boys. Carters Barracks was a two-storey brick building with heavy iron bars on the windows. An ill-boding high wall began at the side of the building and wrapped around, enclosing the yard. It had been built in 1819 to house carters and brickmakers so they could be located closer to their work. Further buildings were added later to accommodate the boys. A high wall ran through the yard to separate the boys from the men. The yards were a hodgepodge of sheds that had various uses such as stables, a saddle room, solitary confinement cells, kitchens, privies, sheds for the carpenters, wheelwrights and smiths and a small leisure area for the men. The only time the boys were exposed to the men was during work assignments.

Inside, the boys were separated into two classes. Each class had its own room but the layout was the same in each. Mess tables lined the front of the rooms allowing the boys a view of the road as they ate their rations. The back of the room had sloping walls where the boys slept. The first class boys enjoyed a cup of tea for breakfast, with a pound of meat and bread, and soup for dinner. They slept on mattresses and were given blankets. The second class boys were only given one meal a day. At night they slept on boards with a coarse India blanket to keep them warm.

During summertime they were woken at sunrise and marched to their workplaces. At around 9 a.m. they returned to the barracks to break for an hour for breakfast. At sunset they ceased working for the day and were also given an hour for dinner. In winter they would muster and have breakfast first before trudging to their workplaces.

John must have been terribly unhappy there, as he made several escape attempts resulting in severe punishments. In most cases, he was subjected to lashings with the cat-o-nine tails and would have been assigned to the second class. Convict children who misbehaved were often sentenced to lashes. They usually received 12 to 36 lashes across their backside or breech as it was called then. When a child turned fourteen years of age they were no longer considered children and would be punished like an adult.

Punishments for adults really varied and could be very harsh. An adult could receive hundreds of lashes.

Over the course of just two months John was lashed on four separate occasions and after each time he ran away. Sometimes it was only a matter of a few days since the last lot of lashes before he was whipped again. It must have been excruciatingly painful as his wounds would not have had time to heal before the next lot were administered. Clearly a testament to how pitiful his existence was at Carters Barracks and his desperation to get away from there. In the end, the authorities realised flogging him was having no effect, so they sentenced him to eleven days in solitary confinement where he received only bread and water.

When still he failed to conform he was sent to the Hyde Park Barracks where government officials labelled him a 'troublesome runaway' and decided to move him from Carters Barracks to the Phoenix Hulk. The hulk served as a floating prison, which was common for old ships that were too old to handle the high seas anymore. They were moored in the harbour and freed up some of the overcrowding problems in prisons and convict barracks both in Sydney and other British colonies.

During his time on the Phoenix Hulk John rebelled again, destroying a blue cloth jacket, which was probably part of his uniform, and was punished with 25 lashes by the Superintendent of the ship. However, the Superintendent realised that repeated punishment was not going to have a lasting effect, so he sent John to Port Macquarie with instructions for the Police Magistrate that he be put to work and taught to read. He also requested that the Reverend pay him frequent visits and give him religious instruction and advice.

Port Macquarie had originally been founded by Governor Lachlan Macquarie, who needed an alternative location for the growing number of convicts being sent from Britain. He made the site a colony for the secondary punishment of reoffending convicts in 1821. However, when John arrived it had become a town for free settlers, with a dwindling convict population. Port Macquarie had proven to be an easy post for convicts to escape, so they ceased sending them there. The government only sent convicts who were considered special cases such as lunatics, invalids and 'gentlemen convicts' that only performed light duties.

A year later John became seriously ill and was sent to Port Macquarie Hospital. Sadly, he died on 23 July 1836; the cause of death was not recorded. He was buried at the local cemetery two days later. He was only about fourteen years old. The cemetery remains today, though his grave is unmarked.

James Frazer

Ship: Albion
Approximate age on arrival: 19 years old
Crime: Privately stealing
Sentence: Death commuted to life
Date arrived: 14 February 1827

James Frazer was a fair, freckled, brown-haired, blue-eyed boy of nineteen years. He had been living in a dwelling house when a fellow lodger, Mr Robert Ferguson, accused him and another boy, Jobbins, of stealing articles of clothing and money from his room. Both boys were arrested and faced trial at the Old Bailey, London's Central Criminal Court, and were sentenced to death. Luckily for Frazer, two witnesses stepped forward and gave him a good character reference and he was spared the hangman's noose. His sentence was changed to transportation for life. Jobbins was not so lucky.

When Frazer arrived in the new colony he was young, fit, educated and he had a skill: shoemaking. About four years into his sentence he was working in a shop when he met Ann Quigley the daughter of a merchant. Frazer must have made a very good impression on her family for they allowed their nineteen year old daughter, who was a free citizen, to marry this young convict man with a life sentence. Frazer then applied to the government for permission to marry Ann and it was granted in February 1831. Frazer and Ann were married later that year.

The Quigley family's good opinion of Ann's choice of husband quickly dissolved though. In November of the same year, James Quigley, Ann's brother, accused Frazer of embezzling over three hundred pounds in treasury bills. Quigley had left the treasury bills in the care of his sister and brother-in-law to mind for him. Frazer and Ann claimed that their house had been broken into whilst they were at church and the treasury bills stolen. The case went to trial and Frazer was the first convict to be granted bail, however, he was ultimately charged with the theft. James Quigley was not without fault though – at the time of the theft he was preparing to sneak out of Sydney and on to Hobart, leaving numerous debts in his wake.

Two years later Frazer began planning his own escape from Sydney. At the time he was working as a dealer and managed to collect a large amount of property on credit. He then sold the properties at a very low rate for cash. With his newly acquired money and a forged document claiming to be a free settler, he was able to obtain a ticket from Customs House on board the *Mail* which was sailing to London. The authorities didn't learn of his cunning escape until after the ship had set sail. An urgent message was sent to London, which arrived just before the *Mail* reached its destination.

Officer Ellis, who had chased Frazer all the way to England, boarded the *Mail*, but Frazer had managed to alight before he got there. However, he was able to apprehend Frazer a few days later as he came out of his mother's house. He had on him a large sum of money which was seized.

Frazer was transported straight back to Sydney where he faced further sentencing.

It was decided that the money found on Frazer should be divided amongst his creditors. Several ads were printed in the local rag, the *The Sydney Gazette and NSW Advertiser* asking for anyone who was owed money by Frazer to apply for compensation. Meanwhile, Frazer received a life sentence to work in irons and transferred to Goat Island.

Goat Island was a secondary punishment site for reoffending convicts. It was also where they stored gunpowder and explosives. The Island had been originally inhabited by the Gadigal people and was known by them as Me-mel. It had been the home of Bennelong and Barangaroo. During the 1830s the convict work gangs were put to work on the island building the Queen's Magazine. They quarried sandstone from the island to build it, which was back-breaking work. It's likely that Frazer worked on this building which stills stands today.

On 12 March 1842, he was awarded a Ticket of Leave and was assigned to the district of Yass.

Five years later, on the 30 October 1847, Frazer was given a Pardon, making him a free man. However, he was not allowed to return to England. He would have been about 39 years old by this time.

Robert Hudson

Ship: John (4)
Approximate age on arrival: 30 years old
Crime: Stabbing a woman
Sentence: Life
Date arrived: 7 February 1837

In a back alley called Barrack Lane in Croydon, England, in November 1835, Robert Hudson slipped out of the shadows and startled Elizabeth Levi. The pair were former lovers who had recently parted ways. Elizabeth left Hudson, moving out of their place to live with some of her friends. Hudson approached Elizabeth with open arms and she felt no fear as he led her into his embrace. Seconds later Elizabeth felt two painful blows to the neck. Her hands immediately flew to her wounds, the shock sent her falling to the ground.

When she came to, she found herself in her friend's home. The doctor informed her that she had been stabbed and said she was lucky to have survived. Hudson had only just missed an artery which would have surely caused her death. Hudson was arrested and the incident went to trial a few months later. In his defence, Hudson claimed to have been driven to such rage as Elizabeth had left him with numerous debts and her sister had verbally abused him. Elizabeth's behaviour during the trial also helped Hudson's defence. She behaved so outrageously that the judge asked for the removal of all minors from the courtroom as he felt that her manner and statements would leave them with a 'moral taint'. The jury convicted him but showed mercy by acquitting him of intent to murder due to the woman's 'bad character and the provocation given.'

At the time of his arrest authorities described him as being 5 foot 4 ½ inches tall with brown hair, grey eyes and a sallow complexion. He had a pock-pitted face which was most likely a sign of an earlier bout with smallpox. His arms were covered in scars and warts and the location of these were meticulously detailed. Hudson was originally from Kent and had worked as a Porter. He could read and write, which made him quite a well-educated man for those times.

He arrived in Sydney in 1837 aboard the ship *John* and was assigned to the General Hospital as a gatekeeper. The hospital, which still stands today, is located in Macquarie Street, situated right next to the Hyde Park Barracks. The façade of the hospital still remains today, but it has now become three separate properties which include Parliament House, The Sydney Eye Hospital and The Mint. The location of the hospital was chosen by Governor Lachlan Macquarie for its elevated position, which allowed a breeze to flow through the hospital. The medical opinion of the time was that a miasma could spread disease, so many hospitals were built on hills. The hospital is often referred to as the 'Rum Hospital', as Macquarie paid the builders with a three-year monopoly on the importation of rum.

For four years Hudson kept a low profile. Life in Sydney seemed to agree with him. He was considered a good worker who was attentive to his duties. However, in 1841 he became sullen after hearing that a fellow convict by the name of Dean Channery West had warned some convict women working nearby that he had been transported for stabbing a woman. Hudson was enraged by the comments. On the morning of 15 September 1841, Mr Neary, the local baker, upon making his usual delivery of bread, discovered West in bed with a large gash to the head, lying in a pool of his own blood. He was still alive but only just hanging on.

Neary notified Dr Croft, who was in charge at the hospital, and a search was conducted. Dr Croft found an axe in the kitchen dripping with blood. It had chunks of human hair on it. After questioning several members of staff, Samuel Huggly, James McLean and Robert Hudson were taken into custody on suspicion. All three men were prisoners of the Crown and were assigned to Dr Croft at the Hospital.

West lingered on for several days until he finally passed away on Saturday, 18 September 1841. During that time he was not able to give any indication as to who had attacked him. The following day Robert Hudson made a full confession at the Hyde Park Barracks. When explaining his motive for the attack he said, 'Dean West and I have often had words, and I have told him that he had better not be reporting my crime about the place in the way he was doing, and he has told me, in reply, that a man like me had no business being about the place.' During the trial, however, Hudson denied making any confession and pleaded 'not guilty'.

In October, a jury was selected and their names were printed in the paper. The inquest was held at the Three Tuns Tavern on the corner of King and Elizabeth Streets, Sydney. Several witnesses were called, Mr Neary, Dr Croft, James McLean and the two convict women Smith and Johnston, who were allegedly told by West of Hudson's crime. Hudson represented himself and had the opportunity to cross-examine the witnesses, though he remained mostly quiet during the trial, choosing to question only one witness.

The Prosecution painted Dean Channery West's character as upstanding, being a well-educated man from a good family and very respectably connected. He had been assigned to the hospital as a clerk and assistant dispenser and was working towards a career in medicine. His sentence of forgery was downplayed.

When the convict women, Smith and Johnston, came to the stand, they both denied any knowledge of Hudson or his crime. In the closing argument, the Prosecution suggested that the prisoner had imagined West's comments. The jury quickly came back with the verdict of guilty. Hudson broke down in tears when the judge read out loud his sentence of death. He was led away in handcuffs to the new gaol in Darlinghurst.

On October 29 1841, Robert Hudson and another prisoner by the name of George Stroud were executed for wilful murder. Around five to six hundred people attended the hanging. Executions often attracted huge crowds as they were looked upon as a source of entertainment. At nine o'clock in the morning the prisoners were taken from their cells and led to the new drop that had been specially constructed for their execution. Both men were clutching a bible.

When they reached the scaffold they were led in devotion by members of the clergy. The ropes were adjusted and soon after both men became the first men to be hanged at the new gaol.

George Vigers

Ship: Florentia
Approximate age on arrival: 22 years old
Crime: Stealing a watch & shoes
Sentence: 7 years
Date arrived: 3 January 1828

In the 1800s when certain politicians in the House of Commons argued that a convict could not be rehabilitated, they would have had characters like George Vigers in mind. Vigers was a 'flash man', meaning he was an experienced criminal. He was in and out of trouble his entire life till he was eventually hanged for murder. During his short lifetime, he had received nearly every kind of punishment the courts could dish out. He had been imprisoned in gaols both in England and New South Wales. He had been lashed hundreds of times, been shackled on the iron gangs, sent to a secondary punishment site and spent time in solitary confinement on reduced rations.

Vigers claimed that he turned to a life of crime at the age of nineteen when he began his career with petty theft. It wasn't until he was twenty-two years old though that he was caught stealing a watch and shoes and sentenced to seven years transportation. He had grown up in Davenport in Greater Manchester. At the time of his arrest, he was 5 foot 2 ½ inches tall, with dark brown hair and hazel eyes. He would have been seen as an ideal candidate for transportation as he was young, had learned a trade, and had experience working as a shoemaker. Vigers arrived in Sydney in 1828 having sailed on the ship *Florentia*.

After being processed at Hyde Park Barracks, Vigers was assigned to Edward Smith who resided in Parramatta. Vigers made numerous attempts to run away. He even forged a pass allowing him to roam free, but it didn't fool police and he was apprehended and sent back. His persistent attempts to escape landed him in an iron gang. Life in the iron gangs was rough.

The men were shackled together doing backbreaking work such as clearing trees and breaking rocks to build roads, with half rations plus bread and water. At night about twenty men were locked together in wooden caravans that were windowless and extremely cramped. The men slept on narrow sleeping shelves and there was only one urinal between them. The caravans became like ovens in the summer heat and would have been horrendous for the men inside.

The only way to escape the caravans and the iron gangs was to bribe the guards, which is what Vigers must have done, as after only a few months on the gang he managed to escape. When he was apprehended he was sentenced to another fifty lashes. And so his life went on – escape, freedom, apprehension, punishment. Over and over again, punishment after punishment, that never broke him but only made him more determined to escape for good. The problem was that in order to survive on his own he needed money and food, which would inevitably lead him to commit crimes such as highway robbery, forgery and theft. This would invariably get him caught.

Eventually, he was sentenced to a penal settlement that had a reputation of being a place worse than death – Norfolk Island. Instead of the island rehabilitating Vigers, it allowed him to forge new contacts with like-minded individuals. Vigers was later transferred to Hyde Park Barracks where he was reunited with other convicts who had suffered time on Norfolk Island, Burdett and Martin. They also had a mate, Rankin, who had a Ticket of Leave and was residing in Kent Street. Rankin had also experienced the horrors of Norfolk Island.

Together they hatched a plan to rob Mr Noble and his family on Clarence Street. On Sunday, 26 May 1844, when they were supposed to be attending church, they managed to slip out and discard their convict uniforms to reveal their civilian clothing which they wore underneath. They met at Rankin's house where they armed themselves with a pistol, shot and powder and knives that had been purchased beforehand, and sat, waiting and drinking till night fell. Around half past six, they decided it was time to make their move and they headed to Mr Noble's house.

Mr Noble was in his sitting room enjoying a quiet evening with his wife and her thirteen year old sister Violet when there was a knock at the door. When Mr Noble answered the door he was handed a letter by Vigers. Mr Noble moved into the house so that he could read the letter under the light of a candle. Vigers, Burdett and Martin followed him inside and Vigers pulled the pistol on Noble's wife. Mrs Noble let out a blood-curdling scream, Mr Noble rushed Vigers, trying to seize the gun, and during the scuffle, Mrs Noble's younger sister had the sense to race for the back door and escape. It had been Burdett's job to secure all the exits, but everything had happened so fast - he hadn't been quick enough.

As Violet fled across the street to the safety of their neighbour Mr Wilson's house, Noble and Vigers continued to wrestle and Noble managed to knock the gun out of his grip. Vigers reached into his pocket for his shoemaker's knife and stabbed Noble in the hand and just under the ribs. Burdett came to the aid of his friend and the two made their escape out the back door. Noble used the last of his strength to seize Martin. Seconds later Wilson and his friend Phillips raced across the street and into the house to find Mr Noble lying in a pool of blood on the floor, grasping Martin who was sitting there in a state of terror and shock, while a distraught Mrs Noble, bent over her husband, also holding Martin. Mr Noble was taken upstairs to his bedroom where he lay till he died the following evening.

Vigers and Burdett were apprehended and put in gaol to await their trial. At the trial Vigers, Burdett and Rankin were found guilty and sentenced to death. During the trial Rankin fainted in the dock and later died in prison from '… fear and a conscience affrighted at the enormity of his crimes.' Martin was spared the noose but was sentenced to a further 10 years.

On 13 August 1844 Burdett and Vigers stepped up to the scaffold at Darlinghurst Gaol. The drop had been erected at the front of the gaol. Burdett seemed extremely anxious as to what lay ahead, but Vigers was described as hardened to his fate. Before the noose was placed around their necks Vigers addressed the crowd: 'In the situation in which I now stand - not knowing where I am going to, or what I am to suffer, I feel it my duty to say a few words with respect to the old man, Rankin. I solemnly declare that he had no knowledge - no idea - where we were going or what we were going to do on the night we left his house and I do declare that I had never been in his house - never seen or spoken to him - until the day on which we did the murder.' He then bowed to the crowd and stepped back so the noose could be adjusted. He turned to Captain Innes and asked him not to forget what he had told him earlier about Hyde Park Barracks. Both Burdett and Vigers had told the captain about the criminal activity within the Barracks and how it had influenced them in committing their crimes. Vigers kept his composure till the end.

Alexander Green

Ship: Countess of Harcourt
Approximate age on arrival: 22 years old
Crime: Stealing cloth
Sentence: Life
Date arrived: 12 July 1824

Born in Holland to two circus performers, Alexander Green spent his childhood and early manhood travelling around Europe with his parents, working as a circus tumbler. He had blonde, almost white, hair, with pale blue eyes and a pale complexion. When he was 22 years old he was caught stealing cloth from a shop in Salop, England and was sentenced to transportation for life. His years spent performing acrobatics had made him very fit and muscular and when he arrived in Sydney on the *Countess of Harcourt* he was quickly snapped up as a convict labourer by the emancipist

William Hutchinson. Green only lasted three weeks in this position before he was returned to the Hyde Park Barracks in Macquarie Street.

By a stroke of luck, in May 1825, Green was notified that His Majesty had reduced his sentence from life to seven years. A few months later he was assigned to Reverend Samuel Marsden, who was both hated and feared by convicts for his cruelty and the severe sentences that he handed down from his work on the bench. His bad reputation amongst convicts had come about in 1800 when he near flogged a convict man to death in the pursuit of wringing a confession out of him. However, Green's luck followed him, as shortly after he was assigned to Marsden he was granted a Conditional Pardon. Green soon left Marsden and returned to Sydney to find work.

In 1826 Green stood as a witness in a case. From then on Green was viewed by his community as a police informant, which was one of the worst labels you could have in Sydney at the time. This could have been what led Green to take up the position of scourger or flogger. It was a lucrative position, as convicts would bribe the scourger to lay the lash lightly and to avoid major organs such as the kidneys so as to prevent lifelong damage. The lash generally consisted of nine lengths of rope with six knots in each. Green spent his time going between the Barracks and the old gaol on the corner of George and Essex Streets.

For reasons unknown, in 1827 Green had given up his position as scourger and had travelled up the coast, living and working in Port Stephens. On 16 April the *The Sydney Gazette and NSW Advertiser* reported that Green had been given the position of Honorary Constable. His rise from convict thief to police officer was short lived though, as two months into the job Green was dismissed for assisting his drunken convict friend John Maher in a brawl. Disgraced from his position Green returned to Sydney.

When the Hangman, Henry Stain, died in 1828 Green was appointed the official 'Finisher'. Green received a salary of 15p 14s.2d a year and the title 'Public Executioner of Sydney Town and the Colony of NSW'. This gruesome job required him to be on call six days a week, with Sunday as a rest day as no hangings were performed on the Sabbath. He was required to travel all over New South Wales to perform his duties. When the new prison Darlinghurst Gaol was opened in 1841, Green was given a whitewashed hut on the eastern side of the exterior of the gaol. The prison still stands today but is now used as the National Art School and the area where Green's hut was is now called Greens Park.

The executioner's role was not only emotionally taxing but physically and mentally demanding too. A 'Finisher' had to have knowledge of the anatomy, be able to gauge a man's weight and have the physical strength to control his victims. There was an art to hanging a man and it was usual for an executioner to visit the victim in gaol before the hanging to get a sense of their weight and the rope length necessary to complete the task. There were several types of knots that were used before the government regulated the practice. Every hangman feared calculating the weight incorrectly and causing the victim a slow strangulation or beheading them. Green's first hanging was a disaster. He was to hang three men. Two of the men met their death instantly, but the third poor fellow's rope snapped half way and he fell to his feet. The man's name was William Smith, and he had to wait and watch the other two while the required time passed before he was strung up again and successfully hanged.

Hangings were public affairs and were seen by many as a type of entertainment. The newspapers reported it. The crowds loved it. There was usually some drama – Green was sent all over New South Wales to perform his duties and in August 1830 he was in Windsor for the hanging of a seventeen year old bushranger, Thomas Tiernan. When asked if he had any final words Tiernan exclaimed to the crowd, whilst looking directly at Green, 'O yes! We must go together.', and with the noose secured around his neck, he lunged at Green and together they fell off the platform. Whilst Tiernan strangled to death, Green got to his feet and realised that his arm had broken in the commotion.

Public Executioner was far from a glamorous job – it was dangerous and, along with a broken arm, Green received a lot of abuse from the newspapers and the general public. He was verbally abused in the streets. The newspapers called him a 'monster'. One particularly bad incident occurred on his return from Port Macquarie where he'd hanged a number of offenders. Whilst on board a schooner, he was accosted by prisoners who recognized him as the executioner. They attacked Green with an axe, striking him down the side of his face, which left a terrible gaping wound that saw him permanently disfigured with a scar that covered one whole side of his face.

About a month after the attack Green received news that he was now a totally free man and could call himself an emancipist. This meant that he was able to move back to England if he so desired. Few convicts returned home after earning their freedom though. For many, the journey home was too arduous, expensive, and Sydney promised a fresh start, with the possibility of becoming more than they ever could have dreamt of back in England. Many convicts were issued land, started their own businesses and became quite successful. For whatever reason, Green decided to stay in Sydney.

The attack had left him hideously scarred and did nothing to help him find love. When he was rejected by a woman in October 1832, Green was so devastated that he tried to take his own life. A friend was passing and saw Green, cutting him down in time. The *Sydney Herald* reported the incident, expressing regret that Green was not successful in his attempt.

In 1835 Green struck out again. He had become infatuated by a laundress named Ester Howell who had recently become a widow. He attempted to gain her affection by showering her with gifts and showed up to her apartment, which she shared with her two children, one night unannounced. When she refused him he flew into a rage and shouted at her so loudly that the constables were alerted and arrested him. A court granted him bail and as soon as he was released he went straight back to Mrs Howell's. This time he was thrown into the very prison for which he worked and there he remained until he was released again with a warning to stay away from her.

Green's love of drinking increased and so did his bungled hangings and his arrests. He was charged with all manner of offences such us stealing a saddle, malicious injury to property, and more than one assault on a woman. Drunkenness was always at the root of every incident. He would spend time in gaol but then be released as soon as the government required his skills. One woman dropped all charges as he had been so good to her and her children in the past. Over time, the executions, his excessive drinking and the constant abuse that was hurled at him from the public and newspapers of the day must have played their part in the decline of his mental health, for he was declared insane. Green was sent to Tarban Creek Lunatic Asylum where he lived out the rest of his days.

Mary Morgan

Ship: Neptune
Approximate age on arrival: 27 years old
Crime: Stealing 38 'slippons' of hempen yarn
Sentence: Death commuted to 14 years
Date arrived: 27 June 1790

Mary Morgan, known to all as 'Molly', was an impressive, colourful character. She was fearless, bold, charitable, daring and ambitious. She was the type of person that used her strength, determination and willpower to rise above the ashes. She was a survivor and a pioneer. Molly Morgan's name became synonymous with Maitland in New South Wales. Through hard work and dedication, she became a very wealthy and successful woman — a large landowner, publican and farmer.

Molly was born in Diddlebury, England and named Mary Jones by her parents David and Margaret. Her father worked as a fox and rat catcher in Corfton. Molly attended school briefly and became a dressmaker. She blossomed into a beautiful young woman and caught the eye of a farmer named Gough. When Molly fell pregnant with his child, he refused to marry her as she lacked the social standing that he felt deserving of. She later gave birth to their daughter and named her Mary. It wasn't long before she met and married William Morgan. The two set up home in a cozy cottage in Cold Weston and a baby boy was soon welcomed into their family.

A few years later the pair were arrested for stealing thirty-eight slippings of hempen yarn after their cottage was searched. Hempen yarn was a popular product used to make ropes, sails and sheets. When the yarn was discovered in their home, the couple were seized by police, and so began their journey to Sutton Court to await their trial. However, somewhere along the way, William managed to escape leaving Molly to deal with the consequences of their actions. Sutton Court was the house of Reverend John

Powell, a man Molly knew well. It was a small town where nothing went unnoticed and gossip was rife. Molly had been baptised by the Reverend and he had married her to William. The shame she felt must have been unbearable, for that night she tried to take her own life.

Meanwhile, as William was hot-footing it across Shropshire he came across a group of soldiers that either forced him into joining the Corps or William had the foresight to do it himself. By doing so, he avoided a probable sentence of death. By some divine twist of fate, or perhaps William's insistence, he and Molly found themselves being transported to New South Wales on the same ship, the *Neptune* - one as a soldier, and one as a prisoner of the Crown. Molly had received a sentence of death that was commuted to fourteen years transportation.

The *Neptune* was one of the Second Fleet's ships. Unlike the First Fleet, this fleet had been commissioned, and the company who were rewarded with the task of transporting the next batch of convicts were only paid to take them, there being no stipulation that they were to be transported alive and in good health. The atrocities that occurred on board would make anyone sick to their stomach. Rations were reduced, convicts were shackled and not allowed on deck. One third of the convicts on board died due to conditions that they endured on this journey. The lucky few that arrived alive were suffering from scurvy, typhoid and dysentery. Their skin was crawling with lice and clothing and blankets were covered in their own filth. The smell of the living quarters below deck was so offensive that Reverend Richard Johnson 'could scarcely bear it'.

An anonymous female convict, who had been fortunate enough to travel on the *Lady Juliana*, commented on the arrival of the *Neptune* – '*they were almost dead, very few could stand, and they were obliged to fling them as you would goods, and hoist them out of the ships, they were so feeble, and they died ten or twelve a day when they first landed …*'. The Reverend Richard Johnson described the scene: '*The landing of these people was truly affecting and shocking; great numbers were not able to walk, nor to move hand or foot; such were slung over the ship side in the same manner as they would a cask, a box, or anything of that nature. Upon being brought up in the open air some fainted, some died upon deck, and others in the boat before they reached the shore. When come on shore many were not able to walk, to stand, or stir themselves in the least, hense some were led by others. Some creeped upon their hands and knees, some were carried upon the backs of others.'*

Molly's resilience and strength were tested during this time. Although it would have been a harrowing journey and many didn't survive, she did. The fact that she was the wife of a soldier and would have shared his quarters and rations, no doubt helped her immensely, but she still would have arrived gaunt and weak. Once in Port Jackson, they continued living as man and wife. She would have been treated better than the other convict women and lived quite freely. However, the relationship quickly turned sour. Rumours spread that Molly was having an affair with William's reporting officer Captain Nepean. William also began an affair with his neighbour Ellen Frazer, a married woman.

With her marriage in tatters and her children on the other side of the world, Molly began planning her escape back to England. She still had eight years left to serve. In 1794 she began circulating rumours that she was going to take off into the bush. She raised as much money as she could by selling her goat and possibly other possessions. Using her connections she stowed away on board the *Resolution*. When the authorities realised she was missing they sent search parties into the bush to look for her but, of course, they came up empty-handed.

Once firmly on English soil, Molly brazenly rushed straight back to her home town to see her children. If caught, she most certainly would have been put to death, but her love and yearning to see her children made it worth the risk. One can only imagine the surprise and elation on the faces of Molly's parents and children when they clapped eyes on her. They hadn't seen her for six long years and thought they never would again. After an emotional reunion, Molly and her beloved children journeyed back to London.

Molly quickly integrated herself and her children in St George's Terrace, East London.

Going by the name of Mary Thomas, she soon met and bigamously married a man named Thomas Mears from Plymouth.

By 1803 her children had grown and left their nest, creating their own lives. Molly found herself in trouble again when their home burnt down and her husband accused her of doing it. She was arrested and faced trial, where she was found guilty and once again sentenced to transportation. She arrived back in Sydney having travelled on the *Experiment*. This was a defining moment for Molly. No longer was her heart in England. Her children had good lives and didn't depend on her any more. This was her chance at a new life and she seized it with both hands. She had a clear advantage, having already lived in Sydney. She knew what items to bring with her on the journey that could potentially put her on the path of becoming a successful businesswoman.

First, she shed the name Mears and went back to being called Molly Morgan. She was already well known by that name anyway. Her former husband had well and truly moved on with

Ellen Frazer. The two now had several children together. She served her time doing various things, which included a stint at the Female Factory, and was moved up the coast to Newcastle. As soon as she had saved the funds though, she rented land off the government and started farming. She purchased a cow and named it 'Kangaroo' and became quite successful.

In 1822 she stole the heart of a young man thirty years her junior and married him. By this stage, she was about sixty years old, but still a desirable match for any man lucky enough to catch her. His name was Hunt and after the honeymoon period died down Molly petitioned the Governor for more land around Wallis Plains and Hunter River. Her small farm had burgeoned to over 300 cattle, 100 sheep, 18 horses and 8 broodmares. Molly was granted 159 acres and the area which is today named Maitland was known as 'Molly Morgan's Plains'.

Her next project was to open an inn which she named 'The Angel' and she was very successful, serving the workers travelling up and down the coast as well as all the locals. Everybody knew and loved Molly. She became an advocate and voice for the convicts. She donated huge sums of money for needy causes, such as schools etc. Her death caused a great sadness and left a huge hole in the community, as no one could ever fill Molly's shoes. Some were so upset they took their anger out on her husband, accusing him of her murder. He was found to be innocent though when the coroner concluded that her death was an accident. Molly was buried at Anvil Creek, near Greta.

Molly lives on today, with many places in the Maitland area being dedicated to her: Mt Molly Morgan, Molly Morgan Ridge, Molly Morgan Drive, Molly Morgan Motor Inn and Molly Morgan Vineyard.

Israel Chapman

Ship: Glory
Approximate age on arrival: 26 years old
Crime: Highway robbery
Sentence: Death commuted to life
Date arrived: 14 September 1818

Israel Chapman was a young man of 24 years, working in a very respectable position in Chelsea as coachman and groom, when he was sentenced to life. He would have been on a good wage and provided board with a reputable family. Coachmen were expected to be clean-shaven, respectable and wear livery which consisted of waistcoats, breeches and double-breasted top-coats, completed with white gloves and a tie. A coachman held the door open for his mistress and was knowledgeable about horses. He was responsible for taking care of his master's valuable carriages, horses, saddles and harnesses, and was often in charge of other staff such as stable boys. It is therefore surprising that someone in this coveted position would risk it all by committing highway robbery.

Israel was caught and sent to Middlesex Gaol. After his trial, he boarded the ship *Glory* which set sail to New South Wales in May 1818. Due to his previous position of responsibility, Israel was spared hard labour and assigned as a police officer at the Lumber Yards. It wasn't uncommon for convicts to be put in positions of trust like this. The military had no interest in performing these types of roles and it offered convicts an incentive to behave, work hard and prove themselves.

In his first post as a constable at the Sydney Lumber Yards, he was put in charge of a large force of convict labourers. The Lumber Yards was situated on the corner of Bridge and George Streets and was established by Governor Phillip early on in the Colony's settlement. There was a huge workforce of labourers, many of whom were highly skilled in areas such as carpentry, blacksmithing, coopering, locksmiths, sawyers, bellow-makers etc. The men were put to work doing all manner of tasks, including creating beautiful highly skilled pieces of furniture for Government House. Some of these pieces are still around today.

During Israel's time there he met Catherine Martin. Catherine was from London and had been sentenced to fourteen years for knowingly having forged bank notes in her possession. She arrived on 30 September 1820 aboard the *Morley*. Just over a month after her arrival, Israel had written to the government for permission to marry Catherine, which was granted. They were married soon after. Israel would have been an attractive prospect for a girl straight off the ship, as he had a good job and marriage would have provided her with some security in a male-dominated population. It would have also saved her from the Female Factory.

In 1822 after only serving four years of his life sentence, Israel was awarded a Conditional Pardon. Around the same time, he was rewarded with a sum of one pound for apprehending a bushranger. Bushrangers were increasingly becoming a problem for the Government. Convicts who managed to escape into the bush often joined gangs and created problems for the settlement. The general public was encouraged, with the promise of financial reward, to apprehend bushrangers. Things were definitely going Israel's way until he got a bit too cocky and sent an 'improper letter' which got him dismissed from his job at the Lumber Yard. Unfortunately, the contents of the letter are unknown. A month later, and still unemployed, Israel put an advertisement in the *The Sydney Gazette and NSW Advertiser* offering his services. He then put in a petition for the mitigation of his sentence, which was successful. He wasn't rehired by the Lumber Yard, but was employed as a district police officer.

Israel took his new position very seriously and was regularly in the papers for apprehending criminals. Various publications described him as 'over-eager' and someone who displayed great 'sagacity'. It was a tough job and Israel was violently assaulted on more than one occasion. As recognition for all of his hard work, in 1827 he was awarded the highly sought after

Absolute Pardon. Israel stayed in Sydney, enjoying his role as a detective which also allowed him to travel around New South Wales investigating different cases. When his wife died at an age when she should have been in her prime, Israel became consumed with grief. Within a month he had boarded a ship back to England.

After a number of years, Israel returned to his life in Sydney with his new bride Mary. The Governor welcomed him back with open arms, granting him a position in the Police Force. However, he ended up on the wrong side of the law again when he was caught stealing and was sentenced to hard labour. He lived a long life, died in 1868. In his final years, his jet black hair had turned grey and his face told the story of many battles. He was scarred and nearly blind in one eye from gunshot wounds. He was laid to rest in a cemetery in Rookwood.

Ann Yates

Ship: Britannia
Approximate age on arrival: 37 years old
Crime: Stealing
Sentence: 7 years
Date arrived: 18 July 1798

When the eighteenth century was drawing to a close, Ann Yates was living and working at the bustling Carnaby Markets in London. She had been hired by a man named Mr Joseph Butler to nurse his sick wife and their three young children. Over a two month period Ann pilfered items from the house – a petticoat here, a cotton handkerchief there, until Mr Butler's suspicions were raised and he alerted a constable. Ann was searched and receipts for the items which had been sold to a local pawn shop were discovered in her pockets.

When the pawn shop owner was questioned he revealed that Ann had been pawning Butler's belongings for two months. Among the loot were linen caps, frocks, tablecloths, two flat irons and sheets. When questioned in court, Ann's defence was: 'I took them to pawn to get the woman more support than her husband allowed her.' Butler argued that his wife was well cared for and in want of nothing. The judge was disgusted that Ann had taken advantage of this family and sentenced her to seven years transportation. By this point in the process, the family had lost their wife and mother as well as one of the three children.

Ann came to Sydney Cove, arriving on board the *Britannia* in 1798. Soon after she arrived she met and married a man named Joseph Morley. They had much in common; they were both convicts carrying a sentence of seven years and had both come from London. It's likely that they knew the same places and possibly even the same people. At any rate, they reminded each other of home, which would have been a huge comfort in such a harsh new existence.

Joseph had been in the colony for many years and had already acquired fifty acres at Prospect Hill. Ann and Joseph lived quite happily together for about ten years, when the relationship began to sour. They had both served their sentences and were free citizens. Ann began planning to leave the colony, a decision she would come to regret. She put an advertisement in the paper letting the public know that she was leaving and needed to settle her financial matters. This was common practice when planning to leave. By this time, she and Joseph had a daughter who was just a baby. She was planning to take the baby with her to start a new life.

Ann paid their passage on board the *Boyd* that was due to set sail to New Zealand. It's doubtful that she was planning to relocate to New Zealand. She was most likely to be on her way back to her homeland. The *Boyd* was stopping in New Zealand to pick up kauri spars and was then taking them to the Cape of Good Hope. Kauri spars were excellent timber for building masts and booms for ships. Also on board was a New Zealand warrior Chief's son. He had been travelling around for some time in the hope of returning to his tribe with iron tools, seal skins and oils.

A few days into the voyage, the resident cook accidentally threw some expensive pewter dinnerware overboard when throwing out a bucket of water. Realising that the punishment could mean his death, he panicked and pointed the finger of blame at the Chief's son. The Chief's son, whose name was Moyhanger, was immediately seized. Moyhanger was outraged, crying out that he should not be degraded in such a manner and reminding them of his high status. The captain disregarded his protests and indignation and commanded that he be flogged, thus sealing the fate of everyone on board.

When the ship finally sailed into the harbour they were met by the people of Warangoa. Moyhanger immediately informed his father of the humiliating treatment he'd received from the captain and the passengers on board the *Boyd*. When he revealed the crusted up scars on his back his father was filled with rage and began to plot his revenge. The following day the Warangoa tribe came aboard the *Boyd* and went on a bloody rampage, clubbing, butchering and bludgeoning their victims. The only people that were spared were Mrs Morley and her baby. Why they were spared is not known. Perhaps she showed a kindness to Moyhanger during the trip. It certainly wasn't because she was a mother with her babe, as other mothers were beaten to death.

We can only imagine the sheer terror Ann must have felt watching the Maoris hack the seventy passengers to death. She would have been rigid with fear, clutching her baby, trying to block out the sounds of people pleading for help as they were bashed, stripped and finally dismembered. Just when she would have thought it was all over she would have seen them take the body parts ashore and watched as a huge fire was built. The ship that was now painted red with blood was set on fire too. Celebrations began that lasted well into the night and Ann would have recoiled in horror as she saw the Maoris roast the body parts and devour them.

The following day three other people were discovered who had carefully hidden away in the recesses of the ship during the massacre.

One a young cabin boy, one a little girl named Betsy and a woman. By then the tribe had had their fill and calmed down considerably. They used the group as leverage and ransomed them for their safe return. Soon a ship arrived to rescue them and they travelled to Lima. When news got back to New Holland and Europe it was met with shock and disbelief. The newspapers warned people against travelling to New Zealand.

Ann never got over her nightmare experience and died soon after reaching the safety of Lima. Her daughter and Betsy were put on the next ship back to Sydney Cove where she was met by her father. The other woman and the cabin boy presumably went on to England. Thankfully Ann's daughter was too young to remember the atrocities that happened that day and she went on to live a happy life in Sydney, working in a school.

Catherine Edwards

Ship: Queen
Approximate age on arrival: 28 years old
Crime: Unknown
Sentence: 7 years
Date arrived: 26 September 1791

Catherine Edwards, who preferred being called 'Mary', travelled to Port Jackson from Ireland on board the *Queen* in 1791 with her two year old son John, after receiving a sentence of seven years. Shortly after their arrival, they were transferred to Rose Hill. Once there, they were issued with provisions such as food, clothing, tools and bedding. Sadly, John died. Consumed with grief, pregnant Mary made the desperate decision to escape across country, through heavy bushland that was so unfamiliar to her.

With twenty other Irish men and women, Mary slipped out of the camp undetected at the beginning of November 1791. The group believed that China was within walking distance – just over some mountains and across a river. The first sighting of the escapees was made not far from camp by a settler who had asked the group where they were headed. When they revealed their plan to walk to China, he tried to talk them out of it, explaining their geographic mistake, but none would hear of it. Troops were sent to turn them back, but they were unable to find them and returned to camp. It wasn't long before most had turned back due to hunger and the rest were eventually found and brought back by force.

Mary gave birth to another son whom she named Thomas Driscoll Edwards, but he died before he was six months old. A few years later, Mary met and married William Yardley, a convict with a life sentence for robbing a shop in south London. He had arrived with the Second Fleet on the *Surprise* in 1790. William and Mary built a life together in Toongabbie where William had acquired some land. It was there that they started their family of four children Edward, Ruth, Mary and William.

On Wednesday, 4 December 1805, William and Mary were in bed together when a fire broke out in their home. William got his wife and children out of the house but ran back inside to seize some of their belongings, when the roof collapsed around him. He didn't survive the accident. When news of the tragedy spread, many speculated on how the fire began. Some thought it was lightning, others blamed the natives and some pointed the finger squarely at Mary.

Mary was extensively questioned by Mr Arndell, a Magistrate, and was taken to the county gaol. A trial began which took place in March 1806 and a sentence wasn't reached until April. William and Mary's servant Henry Murray had also been questioned and taken into custody as a murder suspect. William's body was put on display for the jurors and a startling discovery was made; he had a bandage on his head that was covering a large hole in his skull that had been stuffed with bandages. How the bandages got there was never determined and many speculated that the murderer bandaged William's head to hide a fatal blow. However, it could not be proven if the hole was made from building materials coming down on him or someone hitting him. The jurors came to the conclusion that there was not sufficient evidence to convict and released Mary and Henry.

This would not be the only murder trial that Mary was involved in. Unfortunately for her, the next murder case was to be her own. In 1818, Mary's lifeless body was discovered not far from her home in Portland Head. She had been dead for several days. There was a wound to the back of her head and a stick lying next to her was covered in blood. Richard Hayman, her son-in-law, was brought in for questioning.

Richard along with his wife and children had been living with Mary up until recently when there was an argument and Mary asked him to leave. Richard had been described as a 'mild and gentle' man with a sincere affection for his wife and children. It was only when he spoke of his separation with his wife that he became agitated.

There was an investigation and a trial but Richard was acquitted as there was no evidence to tie him to the murder.

Ann Birmingham

Ship: Marquis Cornwallis
Approximate age on arrival: 21 years old
Crime: Felony deer skins
Sentence: 7 years
Date arrived: 11 February 1796

Ann Birmingham's family kept *The Sydney Gazette and NSW Advertiser* and other newspapers in print with one strange tragedy after another. Even Henry Lawson, the famous poet, made one of them the subject of his poem 'Ghost at the Second Bridge'. Their first mention was on 19 June 1808 when Ann's baby to John Hopkins was horrifically scalded with boiling water in an accident. The couple were in their home at The Rocks when the baby's frock caught the spout of their kettle which was boiling away on the fire. The baby was severely burned and died a few days later.

Ann and John had met and married soon after Ann's arrival in Sydney in 1796. They were to have several children together. John also had a criminal record and was sent to New South Wales in 1791 on board the *Matilda*. When he met Ann, he had nearly completed his seven year sentence. John was self-employed, working as a labourer, and Ann worked as a housekeeper. The next time a Hopkins appeared in the newspaper was in 1836 when their daughter Mary was involved in a bizarre murder/suicide.

Mary had been married to a chap named William James since 1820. The couple were living on Bathurst Rd in a place called Twenty Mile Hollow, which is known today as Woodford. William had illegally built a hut on Crown property and had been living there for many years with his wife and children. According to Quaker missionaries, Backhouse and Walker, the dwelling that the Jameses resided in was 'a miserable hovel, adjoining a public house which we declined entering some weeks before from the wretched appearance of the place.' William was rumoured to be of bad character – selling sly grog much to the annoyance of his neighbour, Mr Pembroke, who owned the inn next door. Mary also had a reputation as being the local drunk.

According to a neighbour, Mary had been miserable in the marriage for some time. One night she tried to end her life by tying her handkerchief around her neck and to the rafters and kicking a box out from beneath her. When a neighbour discovered her she was immediately cut down much to Mary's dismay. Mary abused the neighbour for not minding their own business and leaving her alone. It was said that Mary then swigged some more rum, pushed the neighbour aside, tied the handkerchief around her neck once again and stepped up onto the box, determined to get the job done.

This time her husband appeared and offered to help her! With their children in the next room, William assisted his wife by kicking the box out from under her. He then grabbed her legs and pulled, using his full weight. When he was satisfied that she was gone, he walked out of the room and into the kitchen, leaving her hanging there. Later, her son saw his mother hanging from the rafters and rushed in to save her but it was too late. The police were notified and William was arrested. He was tried, found guilty and sentenced to death. This sentence was overturned to life and he was sent to Norfolk Island.

Ann's granddaughter, Caroline, was the next to appear in the local newspapers as the alleged murder victim of the ultimate bad boy named John Walsh. Walsh arrived in New South Wales in 1833 with a seven year sentence for housebreaking. He was 5 foot 4 inches tall, with brown hair, brown eyes and a sallow, pock-pitted complexion. Walsh had a seedy, violent, dark past. He was repeatedly in trouble with the law. He'd spent time in prison before being transported and continued a life of crime in New South Wales. Years earlier he had been suspected of repeatedly bashing a man's skull in, but was acquitted of the murder as there was insufficient evidence to convict him. He was also acquitted of murdering a woman and her little boy who had also been bludgeoned to death.

Ann's granddaughter, Caroline, had been married to William Collits for about eighteen months at the time of her death when only seventeen years old. Before she married William though, she had been intimately involved with John Walsh.

During the murder trial, it came out that years ago John Walsh had seduced the then fifteen year old Caroline before seducing her younger sister and marrying her. Caroline went on to marry William Collits who the papers described as having a 'nervous and weak disposition', but he was considered a good catch as he owned property and cattle. However, prior to the murder, Caroline had been separated from William and had moved in with her former lover and her sister. Rumour had it the three were engaged in a *ménage á trios*. But at the time of the murder, there was talk that Caroline was in the process of reconciling with her husband and was planning to move back in with him.

The gruesome murder took place in January 1842 after Caroline and William were having a drink at an Inn with Walsh. The three of them left and wandered in the direction of home when Walsh, without being provoked in any way, exploded with rage and surprised William with a hard punch to the face and rained down vicious verbal abuse at him. Caroline tried to intervene, grabbing Walsh and screaming at her husband to run for his life. She shouted, 'run, run, he has got a stone, and will murder you.' Thanks to Caroline's courage, William was able to escape, not knowing that that would be the last time he saw his wife alive.

Unable to take out his jealous rage on William, Walsh turned on Caroline, a powerless teenage girl fighting against the solid, muscular man. Walsh was drunk and shaking with anger and he attacked Caroline repeatedly. Caroline was later discovered not far from where she was last seen. She was covered in cuts and bruises and her head had been bashed in with a stone that lay beside her. It was covered in her blood and hair. There was also evidence that she had been violated before her death. Walsh was immediately arrested and sent to Bathurst Gaol. He denied having anything to do with it, but he was covered in scratches, indicating that

Caroline had fought for her life. Caroline had also managed to tear bits of his clothing off and they were discovered near her body. The jury found him guilty and sentenced him to death.

Years later, Henry Lawson immortalised Ann's granddaughter, Caroline, by writing a poem about her. It was published in 1891 and is titled 'Ghost at the Second Bridge'. According to local residents of Hartley, Caroline has been seen dressed in black walking along the convict built bridge. She not only scared the people crossing the bridge but also spooked their horses. Henry Lawson, who lived nearby, wrote a sixteen verse poem about her.

> *"She'll cross the moonlit road in haste*
> *And vanish down the track;*
> *Her long black hair hangs to her waist*
> *And she is dressed in black;*
> *Her face is white, a dull dead white –*
> *Her eyes are opened wide –*
> *She never looks to left or right,*
> *Or turns to either side."*

Stephen Little

Ship: Minerva (5)
Approximate age on arrival: 16 years old
Crime: Robbing a shop
Sentence: 7 years
Date arrived: 19 November 1824

Stephen Little was just sixteen years old when he was sentenced to seven years transportation for robbing a shop in the wealthy area of Woodford, London. At the time he was only 5 foot 2 inches tall with brown hair and blue eyes. He didn't attend school, but was employed as a hostler which involved looking after horses at a local inn, probably not the greatest place for an impressionable boy. After being found guilty and sentenced, he spent several bleak months imprisoned in a miserable hulk before setting sail on a ship bound for New

South Wales. He arrived at the end of 1824, having travelled on board the *Minerva 5*.

On arrival, all convicts were supposed to be issued with a woollen jacket, a waistcoat, pair of trousers, stockings, shoes, two shirts and a neck handkerchief. However, this often didn't occur, as was the case with Little. Clothing for convicts had been a problem since colonisation and became a huge expense for the colony. Britain wasn't sending nearly enough for the growing demand. Money was taken from the Police fund to employ women at the Female Factory to make clothing. In the early days, material was sourced from old canvas and sheets found in the stores. Clothing was so scarce it became a form of currency among the convicts. The buying, trading and selling of uniforms became such a problem that the government started stamping all uniforms, bedding, even tools and anything else that could be traded, with a broad arrow to identify it as government property. Anyone caught trading these items faced serious punishment.

Unlike the other boys on the *Minerva* who were sent to the Carters Barracks, Little was assigned to private employment. Convicts privately employed were to have their clothing provided by their employers to ease the burden on the government. Little should have been issued with some much needed clothing by his employer Mr Cooper, but wasn't. He was later sent to Carters Barracks, but even though he was now in rags, the government didn't issue him with anything either. In order to keep warm and decent, he stole a pair of trousers and was punished with twelve days on the treadmill.

The treadmill was a device that was used for punishment as well as grinding grain. From 1825 there were two near Carters Barracks where central station stands today. The larger one was for men only and could fit thirty-six men side by side. It was a difficult and scary punishment, as the prisoners had to keep in time and the wheel moved quite fast – it rotated twice a minute. They had to tread for twenty minutes and then they would be given a twenty minute break. This would continue all day long. If you didn't keep in time you could miss your step and fall into the mechanics of the wheel, facing possible death. One convict reached his arm in to retrieve a coin and was unaware that the men on the other side were about to start treading. He was pulled into the wheel and his head was crushed. He died instantly.

It was a turbulent year that followed for Stephen. He had been shuffled from one employer to the next and had a stint in hospital. A year passed with still no new clothing. He was punished twice for using threatening and abusive language with his superiors and received 25 lashes with the cat-o-nine tails. All his other offences around this time were acts of survival after being neglected by the government. He had been caught stealing peaches with two other boys from the Carters Barracks and he was also caught stealing bedding, both of which were in short supply. He made a considerable mistake, however, in 1831 when he stole clothing, boots and a watch off a private who was so intoxicated that he had fallen asleep in the street. Stephen was sentenced to be exiled yet again, to the penal settlement of Moreton Bay for two years. The convicts there were made to wear leg irons and treated very harshly. There he seems to have settled down as he disappears from the record.

Charles Anderson

Ship: Henry Tanner
Approximate age on arrival: 24 years old
Crime: Housebreaking
Sentence: 7 years
Date arrived: 27 June 1834

Charles Anderson was an educated young man working as a seaman in the Royal Navy. He had a lot of potential and his life was on a positive trajectory until he suffered a severe head injury leaving him brain damaged. His accident left him mentally unstable, without the ability to keep his emotions in check. He lashed out in violent outbursts. His behaviour was unpredictable and irrational. Instead of looking after Charles, the Royal Navy discharged him.

It wasn't long before he was in trouble with the law, arrested for housebreaking. He was shipped off to New South Wales on board the *Henry Tanner*. Charles was twenty-four years old, 5 foot 1 inch tall, with sandy brown hair and grey eyes. His arms and chest were covered in tattoos – probably mementos from his days in the Royal Navy. He had all manner of designs crudely tattooed, from mermaids, anchors, names, dates, letters to hearts with darts and Adam & Eve. He retained some of his boyhood innocence with his ruddy cheeks that were covered in freckles.

Charles was soon sent to Goat Island to work in irons. His behaviour there was extremely volatile. He frequently lashed out, striking fellow prisoners and overseers, earning him extra time on his sentence and lashes with the cat-o-nine tails. The authorities were at a loss to know what to do with him and eventually separated him from the rest of the men. The story goes that he was cruelly chained to a rock on the edge of the island for two long years. The other convicts were warned to keep away from him. His only contact with others was when he was fed with a long pole. He was also seen by ships passing the island. It was said that many took pity on him and threw food to him. He apparently became so malnourished that he was nicknamed 'Bony' Anderson.

After two years he was released from his place on the rock and, not surprisingly, he didn't slot neatly back into society. Still unsure of what to do with him, he was shuffled from one penal settlement to the next – Cockatoo Island, Norfolk Island and Port Macquarie. Charles was at Norfolk Island at the same time as Frederick Mitton. When he began to be bullied and teased by the other convicts the benevolent Captain Maconochie tried using occupational therapy. He separated him from the group and gave him his own responsibilities. Charles was put in charge of the bullocks, where he thrived. His behaviour calmed, he received praise for his good work and conduct, and there was a notable difference in him. Maconochie then promoted him to manage the signal station, which he performed with great care. Unfortunately, he still struggled with mental health issues, despite massive improvements, so he was sent to Tarban Creek Lunatic Asylum for professional help.

Incredibly, after just one year, he was declared sane and released into the general population. A few years later he earned himself a Ticket of Leave, but he reverted to old form and ended up back at Cockatoo Island. He continued to get into trouble with the law, being sent back to Cockatoo Island again in 1854 and then he disappears from the record.

Mary Jackman

Ship: Diana
Approximate age on arrival: 32 years old
Crime: Robbery
Sentence: Death commuted to life
Date arrived: 25 May 1833

At the time of Mary Jackman's arrest, she was working as a mistress in a boarding house. It was located in Goswell Street in the north of London, a street made famous by Charles Dickens in his book *The Pickwick Papers*. On the 26 June 1831 Mr Henry McFarlin, a gatekeeper for the East India warehouses, came to Jackman asking for a room for the evening. McFarlin claimed that after taking his money Jackman and other women working in the house attacked him. According to McFarlin, Jackman had hit him in the eye and the others scratched at his face whilst clawing at his jacket pocket where he kept his money. After shouting 'murder and robbery' at the top of his lungs, the police came and arrested the women. When Jackman was given the opportunity to defend herself in court she proclaimed, 'I am as innocent as a baby unborn - what he has sworn is very false'. The judge did not buy it though and sentenced her to death, however the other women were found not guilty. Her sentence was later changed to transportation for life.

When authorities were preparing the paperwork for her transportation, Jackman told them she had worked as a midwife, nurse and housemaid. Whether this was true is unknown. Midwifery was one of the most sought after and useful skills for the expansion of the colony.

At thirty-two, she had been married and was a little older than the ideal age for transportation, but she was an experienced woman and would be an asset in Sydney. She was only 5 foot tall, with brown hair and grey eyes and had a fair complexion. If she had had a career as a nurse it would have prepared her for the harsh conditions of the life of a prisoner and being a pioneer in a new world.

After a long and arduous journey at sea, she took her first steps on the shores of the mysterious land on the other side of the world on 25 May 1833. Shielding her eyes from the light after what had been nearly six months spent mostly below deck in the dark and dank confines of the ship, she lined up with the other convict women to await her fate. She was looking at a life sentence and had no idea what lay ahead of her. As many of the other women were sent into private work as domestic servants, Mary had already been chosen to work at the Female Factory, where her skills would come to be in high demand.

The Female Factory was a place where unwed mothers could lie-in and deliver their babies. It also served as a place of employment and helped regulate and separate women as well as ease the problem of overcrowding in hospitals. The Female Factory was in use from 1821 to 1847. The building was located next to the river on a four acre block. It had a formidable high stone wall with a moat that wrapped around it. The entire site looked like an austere, foreboding place and proved to be poorly constructed. It must have filled the women with dread when they were forcibly led to it.

The conditions inside weren't much better. There were reports of poor food, no easy water source and scarce medical attention, with at least one case of a woman dying through malnutrition. Pregnant women were assigned to the second class and were not given the same standard of food that the first class women enjoyed. There was no nursery and no fireplace to keep the babes warm. Midwives were in short supply and the death rate for children was alarmingly high. Mary worked extremely hard for her eight pence a day and slowly over time conditions improved.

A year into her life in the colony Mary met a man named Joseph Cox. He too had arrived in New South Wales as a convict and was serving a seven year sentence. They soon requested permission to marry but, unfortunately, their request was denied. This was due to the fact that

Mary was already married, her husband being back in England. A couple of months later they tried again and this time their wish was granted. Mary's good behaviour and her invaluable work as a midwife probably helped sway the powers that be in their decision.

Mary didn't return to a life of crime. Her behaviour since coming to the colony had been exemplary. In 1841 she had created a good life for herself in Bathurst and had earned herself a Ticket of Leave. Her relationship with Joseph ended but she married again in 1843 to another convict named Thomas Balcombe, who was serving a life sentence for horse theft. After many years together Mary earned her Conditional Pardon and then she disappears from the record.

William Henshall

Ship: Fortune and Alexander
Approximate age on arrival: Unknown
Crime: Forgery
Sentence: 7 years
Date arrived: 12 July 1806

William Henshall was a skilled silversmith who was arrested for forging currency. In a hopeless attempt to save himself, he ratted on his fellow forgerers, and even worked with the Bank of England to help fight further counterfeiting. However, his betrayal did not earn him a reprieve. He then tried to negotiate his family a passage to New South Wales, but that proved to be fruitless too. He said goodbye to his wife and seven children and arrived in the colony in 1806 with a seven year sentence.

His efforts were to pay off eventually, when in 1813 Governor Lachlan Macquarie heard about William's skills and requested a meeting with him. Macquarie had come up with a solution for the colony's currency problem and he chose William to help him. Macquarie had sourced 40,000 Spanish coins and needed someone with the right skills to punch a hole in the coin to make a holey dollar and dump. He also wanted both parts to be stamped with 'New South Wales 1813'. It was a project he hoped would be finished in a matter of a few months, but it took William over a year. The reason the task proved harder than Macquarie thought was due to having to create machinery for the job.

Macquarie set William up with a workplace in the basement of a government building on the corner of Bridge and Loftus Streets. The holey dollar was worth five shillings and the dump was worth fifteen pence. On some of the coins, William put a tiny 'H' for Henshall which is highly unlikely to have been permitted. Once the machinery was up and running, the coining began to flow.

The first batch of coins were completed in January 1814. Shortly afterwards William's brother arrived in New South Wales as a convicted criminal. He immediately went to work with William to complete more batches. Then his brother's wife and children came and William also took on two female convicts to help finish the job. Clearly, William was getting paid rather well to be able to keep them all.

In 1814 William received permission to marry again. Her name was Sarah Warrell and she had come out as a convict on board the *Sydney Cove* in 1807. She was originally from Leicester and had been sentenced to seven years transportation. Sarah was working as a housekeeper when she met William. Unfortunately, they were only a few years into their marriage when Sarah died. William packed up and left the home they had created together and went back to England where he lived out the rest of his days.

Robert Sidaway

Ship: Friendship (First Fleet)
Approximate age on arrival: 30 years old
Crime: Grand Larceny
Sentence: Death commuted to 14 years
Date arrived: 26 January 1788

Robert Sidaway was a compassionate, generous man with a social conscience who tried to make the colony a better place to live in. He became an important member of the community in early Sydney. He was a baker, providing the colony with bread for the Marines and also sources of entertainment with his pub and theatre. Both were places where all classes of society could come together to unburden themselves from the pressures, hardships and rigours of life in the burgeoning city of Sydney.

In 1782 Robert had been caught stealing a box containing waistcoats, breeches and the like and was sentenced to seven years transportation to the plantations in America. However, before he even reached Newgate gaol Robert made an escape attempt from the Sessions House. He was able to squeeze himself through a hole in the wall and made off down the road with irons on, into a house. When the police knocked on the door Robert answered the door dressed in a green bonnet, petticoat and white bedgown. He thought he had pulled it off, but the policeman recognised his face and arrested him. This time he was sentenced to death, which was later commuted to fourteen years transportation to Sydney Cove.

Robert sailed out on the *Friendship,* which was the smallest ship of the First Fleet and was moored at Botany Bay on 19 January 1788. He disembarked a week later at Port Jackson, which was deemed a more suitable location. By the time Robert had reached Sydney, he had already served about six out of his fourteen year sentence. Six years later he had received an

Absolute Pardon, but instead of returning home to Britain, Robert established his life in Sydney.

The people residing in Sydney found different ways to let their hair down. All classes enjoyed drinking and gambling and found a variety of ways to amuse themselves. There were cockfights, cards, horse and dog racing, cricket and fist fighting to name a few. Convicts would gamble anything they could get their hands on, including the clothes they were wearing. It was not uncommon to see a convict walking back from a card game next to naked. Pastimes such as hunting and fishing were popular and officers had even built a billiard room that was exclusively for their use. Pubs were popping up all over the place and overflowed with people sampling homemade brews which sometimes proved to be deadly concoctions.

Theatrical performances were also a popular source of entertainment. The first play to be performed in the colony was during the celebration of King George III's birthday in 1789. In 1796 Robert had the first theatre in Sydney built using convict labour. It was situated in The

Rocks, right where the Sydney Harbour Bridge stands today. The plays were typical English entertainment. The first opening play was based on 'Othello'. It was called 'The Revenge' and was performed on 16 January 1796.

At first, Robert's theatre filled a great need within the community and was seen as a very positive addition to their ever-growing town. However, it wasn't long before trouble arose. Certain convicts would watch to see who in town was attending the shows and, during the performances, they would rob their houses. It became such a problem that Governor John Hunter ordered the theatre to close only a few years after it had opened. It did open again, but only briefly before closing its doors again.

Perhaps the most important way that Robert gave back to his community was when he and his partner adopted a girl named Elizabeth who the papers described as having a 'mental derangement and bodily infirmity, from a paralytic affection'. She was unable to speak and was totally dependent on Robert and his partner. However, she brought them great joy and was known to be both vivacious and to have a 'placid disposition'. In 1805, at just sixteen years of age, she was rescued from a well that nearly drowned her. She was found head down in the water but was quickly pulled out and resuscitated. Sadly, she died a year later, putting an end to her sufferings.

Robert died only a few years after Elizabeth. His long-term de facto Mary Marshall wrote to Governor Macquarie to try to keep the leasehold on their property, but the request was denied. She did, however, continue as a publican.

Ann Jarvis

Ship: Competitor
Approximate age on arrival: 32 years old
Crime: Larceny
Sentence: 7 years
Date arrived: 10 October 1828

When Ann was arrested for common larceny in 1827 and given a seven year sentence, it was not her first offence. She had previously been in trouble with the law and served a three year sentence in England. This time, however, she was to be transported across the seas. But for Ann, it wasn't all bad news as it meant that she could join her recently convicted husband. Perhaps she even purposely committed a crime to reunite her family when she couldn't afford the passage out to New Holland.

Prior to their convictions, Ann, her husband Thomas and their baby lived in the West Midlands. Ann worked as a cook and Thomas as a shoemaker. Ann was thirty-two years old, 5 foot 3 ¼ inches tall, with brown hair and brown eyes. Her husband was thirty-five and stood at a few inches taller than her, also with brown hair and brown eyes. He had a ruddy complexion and sported several tattoos up and down his arms. Although Thomas had been convicted first, Ann and their baby were transported and arrived in Sydney several months before him. Just before his feet were to be planted on solid ground Ann had broken the law again and been sent to the Female Factory.

Ann was put in the third class which was the worst class to be in at the Factory. Women of that class had been sent there as a disciplinary measure. They were on smaller rations than the other inmates. They were also given menial unpaid tasks such as picking oakum or breaking rocks. Picking oakum involved untwisting ropes which were later used for shipbuilding. The women despised these jobs as not only were they tedious, it really hurt their hands. The fibre was so coarse it dried their skin, leaving them bleeding and sore. Prisoners left to this task often came away with scars and problems with their hands and wrists due to the repetitive hand motions.

If a woman in the third class did not comply with the rules they often forcibly had their head shaved. This was perhaps the most despised punishment, as it robbed them of their femininity and identity and labelled them for a long time until it grew back. This form of punishment was so hated it was part of the reason for the riot in 1831, where inmates seized the matron, held her down and gave her a taste of her own medicine. For this reason, the staff were not keen to be the one to administer the punishment, so they tried to entice one of the prisoners to do it. Ann Jarvis became the new head-shaver at the Female Factory and was about as popular among the inmates as the scourger had been at Hyde Park Barracks.

What became of Ann's child is unknown. Children of convicts were allowed to stay with their mothers in the Factory until they were three years old. Then they were sent to Orphan Schools where they were educated in domestic work for girls and a trade for the boys. There was also the Female School of Industry which was established by Lady Darling in 1826. It too provided girls with training in domestic work designed to make them more employable and less likely to turn to a life of crime like their parents.

By 1831 Ann and Thomas had reunited and brought two more children into the fold. In February they bought a house in Sydney from Mary Harrington. They paid five shillings for the brick home in Kent Street and were to pay Mary eight shillings per week for the duration of Mary's life. Upon her death, they were also obligated to pay for her funeral. It was a great new start for both of them and offered a sense of permanency in the new colony. However, it was short-lived as Ann found herself back in the Female Factory. She was reported a few months later as having absconded.

Ann was in and out of trouble during the early years of her sentence but as time went on she and Thomas settled down and eventually earned themselves Pardons and then Certificates of Freedom.

William Cluer

Ship: Royal Admiral
Approximate age on arrival: 25 years old
Crime: Highway robbery
Sentence: Death commuted to Life
Date arrived: 7 October 1792

William Cluer was sentenced to death in a court in Middlesex, England in 1791. The relief William must have felt when he learned that his sentence was to be commuted to life and that he was to be transported across the seas must have inspired him to turn his life around. He was never in trouble with the law again and became a successful businessman. He arrived on board the *Royal Admiral* in October 1792. The voyage out had been hard, with many on board dying of fever. Many did not set foot ashore at Port Jackson but were immediately taken straight to Parramatta.

William established himself as the first pipe-maker in the colony. Smoking tobacco was a popular pastime with all classes of society. Tobacco crops were planted early on in colonial New Holland. It grew well in this climate but was not as favoured as the imported kind. Still, it was a profitable crop for farmers. Tobacco was distributed amongst the convicts as part of their rations and was probably used as an incentive to work hard.

William created his pipe manufactory at Brickfield Hill. It was a fairly simple process of rolling a clay stem and inserting a piece of wire and then using a mould to create the bowl. The maker often stamped his name, usually along the stem, and the bowls varied from quite plain to the elaborately decorated. Businesses could get their design and name stamped on them. In 1831 a bushranger known as the Wild Colonial Boy was shot in the head and killed. A pipe-maker made a cast of the dead bushranger's head and made a batch of pipes featuring his head as the bowl. It proved to be a very popular design.

The introduction of the first newspaper in New Holland was called *The Sydney Gazette and NSW Advertiser* and it was an aid to William in growing his pipe-making business. The newspaper was first published in 1803. William began placing ads from 1804, announcing when he had completed a new batch of pipes, describing their quality and durability. He sold them at six shillings per gross from Brickfield Hill, where he lived and manufactured the pipes. His business was so successful that within two years he raised his prices to nine shillings per gross, also offering delivery to the buyer's residence.

William's pipes were most likely stocked at the many tobacconists dotted around the colony. Pubs were also likely to have stocked them, as was the case in England. They may have even been labelled with the pub's name. Generally, it is thought that the average pipe would last anywhere from several days to two weeks. It was really dependent on how it was looked after and how delicate the pipe was. The pipes with the longer stems, for example, had a shorter life. Thicker, heavier more robust pipes were designed for labourers. The demand for pipes was so great that many were imported from Scotland and The Netherlands.

William had definitely found himself a successful career, and invested his money in land and property. He already had his home at the Brickfields, which included an outhouse, gardens, a yard and a well. Next, he purchased a dwelling at 15 Castlereagh Street which he rented out to two families. It too had an outhouse, gardens and a yard. He also bought 100 acres of land and a stock run of 30 acres in Bulanaming which was located on the banks of the Cooks River.

His success though, attracted the wrong kind of attention, as his house was broken into in 1808. The thief took a sum of silver and copper coins, a linen shift and some salted pork. William offered a huge reward of two pounds for any information on the theft. Unfortunately, he was robbed on at least two other occasions. He lost some of his livestock – ducks, a drake and two hens from his outhouse. When he then lost several planks of wood, he offered a reward of five pounds.

Between these unfortunate events, William met and married Mary Burfill, a free citizen. Mary arrived on the *Buffalo* and had been working as a housekeeper for a captain. Once married, William taught Mary the business and she went on to become a pipe-maker in her own right. Mary kept the business going when William was on business trips to England. They were together for over ten years until things started to fall apart. In 1823, according to William, she ran off, leaving him no choice but to start divorce proceedings. He put an ad in the paper explaining the situation and claiming to have done nothing to provoke her desertion. He refused to pay any debts she might have incurred.

The following year William died. At the time of his death, he was a free man who was one of the success stories of transportation.

Samuel Wheeler

Ship: Alexander (First Fleet)
Approximate age on arrival: 29 years old
Crime: Grand larceny
Sentence: 7 years
Date arrived: 19 January 1788

Before his conviction, Wheeler was living and working in Kingston-upon-Thames as a brickmaker. He was about twenty-seven years old when he was arrested and charged with grand larceny. He spent nearly two years in gaol before being placed on a ship to New South Wales. He arrived on the *Alexander* and the trip was an eventful one.

Before the *Alexander* had even left England it was plagued with an illness which killed sixteen men. During the voyage there was an escape attempt made by a notorious convict named

John Powers, who later became known as Australia's first bushranger and the man who wounded Pemulwuy an Aboriginal warrior. Powers was also involved in an attempted mutiny on board which was thwarted by a convict informer.

The ship itself had problems with the bilge water rising too high, which caused great illness amongst all classes. During the voyage, a convict fell off the spanker boom into the water and rescue attempts were unsuccessful. On the final leg of the journey they were hit with severe storms which caused great damage to the ship and made many ill. When they finally arrived in Botany Bay many were sent to cut grass to feed the livestock and then ordered back on board to continue to Port Jackson.

After disembarking and settling into life in this strange new country, Wheeler, along with many others, was assigned the task of producing bricks and tiles. Wheeler's previous experience in London earned him the title of Master Brickmaker and he had twenty-one convict men assigned to him. Wheeler was responsible for producing 30,000 bricks and tiles per month. The men not only made the bricks and tiles but had to collect the materials to make them, which involved chopping wood and digging clay. They soon discovered where the best clay could be found and that became the site for the brickfields.

There were five steps to creating a brick. The first was called winning and involved digging for clay and leaving it out in the elements so it would soften a little. The second was called preparation and was considered the most gruelling, arduous and tedious step. This step was often reserved for hardened criminals as a form of punishment. It required convicts to work the clay, picking out any stones and adding water to get the right consistency. When ready, the clay was delivered to the moulding table for the third step, moulding.

The moulding table was called a stool and Wheeler had two tile stools and one brick stool for his team. An assistant would supply him with the right amount of clay and he would then put it into a wooden mould, scraping off the excess with a strike. Beechwood was the best for moulds as clay didn't tend to stick to it as much as other timbers. Sand was often used also to prevent sticking, much like dusting a cake tray with flour. The wooden mould would indent the brick with the broad arrow which identified it as government property.

The next step was drying. The bricks were laid out and men on this step would rotate the bricks, making sure that they weren't warping in the heat. They also scraped the sides to give them a smooth finish. The drying process took two weeks, then they were ready for the final step of burning. The bricks were put in a huge kiln and the master brickmaker was responsible for the tricky process of getting the temperature correct at the right times to ensure the bricks didn't explode or crack. The bricks came out differently depending on the placement within the kiln. The bricks with the best finish were saved for the exterior of the walls.

Wheeler's crew grew over time and so too did his quota. According to Watkin Tench, Wheeler thought the bricks they made were a good quality when compared to the ones produced in London. However, the tiles they were producing had a 'rotten quality' that fell below standard compared to London.

Years later, after serving his time, Wheeler acquired land at the Field of Mars, Hawkesbury and later in life at Windsor. He worked as a labourer his whole life and was last recorded in Evan on the 1828 census as being 79 years of age.

Abraham Lawley

Ship: Layton
Approximate age on arrival: 20 years old
Crime: Stealing a handkerchief
Sentence: 14 Years
Date arrived: 8 November 1829

It was a rainy day in November 1829 when Abraham Lawley stepped ashore leaving his homeland behind forever. He was only twenty years old and had significant relationships that he was leaving behind. One, in particular, was with Ann Pembutton, and Abraham expressed his sorrow at their parting by creating a love token especially for her. Love tokens, or 'Leaden hearts,' were coins that had been smoothed and engraved by convicts facing transportation and given to loved ones as a token of affection. It was a keepsake and memento to mark their imminent separation. Most would never see their loved ones again.

Abraham used a technique called stippling to decorate his token for Ann. This involved using a pin to mark the smoothed coin. On one side he drew a balloon over a gondola with flags with both their initials perhaps representing freedom. On the other side, he fashioned their names, his age, the length of his sentence and the date. His token can be seen on display at the National Museum of Australia.

Abraham was a slender build of 5 foot 6 ½ inches tall, with brown hair and blue eyes. He had two scars, one that ran down the left side of his cheek and the other on the left side of his chin. His complexion was described as ruddy and he had a freckled face. Originally from Birmingham, he had worked as a polisher until he was caught stealing a handkerchief and sentenced to fourteen years transportation. Although he was only young, this wasn't his first trouble with the law. Four years prior he had been convicted of larceny and spent twelve months in prison.

Being transported across the seas did little to reform Abraham. He was in and out of trouble for the next few years until he settled in Goulburn. It was here that he knuckled down and managed to earn himself a Ticket of Leave and eventually a Certificate of Freedom. He even started putting money away in the bank. But this was short-lived, as within a year he was sentenced again for larceny and spent three months in Berrima Gaol.

In 1852 a great flood occurred along the banks of Mulwaree Creek and Wollondilly River around the town of Goulburn where Abraham was living. On Wednesday evening 30 June, there was a torrential downpour, along with powerful, gusty winds that caused the water to rise rapidly. Many of the townsfolk of Goulburn were caught by surprise and failed to evacuate in time. The water rose so high that some families climbed onto the roofs of their homes for safety.

Abraham's neighbours were trapped by the rising waters. Without considering the risk to his own life, Abraham swam to their hut with his horse and led the family, one by one, to a safe place. *The Empire* newspaper described his actions as heroic. The storm passed and eventually the water receded, but the town of Goulburn had been hit hard. Several lives were lost, along with livestock. The mill and brewery also suffered a large loss of stock. The community rallied together to clean up the devastation and to mourn the losses.

Years went by and Abraham found himself on the other side of the law when one of his employees threatened to physically harm him. He had been in this position once before when a young boy of 19 years of age had stolen some horses off his property, but this time Abraham turned to the law for his own personal safety. The offender was Thomas Rowe, a hard looking labourer who loved his drink. In fact, he had 'staggered in drunk' when the case was heard. Abraham claimed that Rowe had threatened to 'knock his teeth down his throat' and dance the 'double shuffle' on him. Rowe was ordered to be locked up.

Not long after the incident Abraham got his publican licence and opened a pub. When he wasn't serving drinks to the locals, he was out at the horse races. Abraham loved sport and his passion for it earned him a spot as a judge. A year later he sold his business and relocated to Braidwood, where he indulged in his love of cricket. He dedicated much of his free time to watching cricket matches and became well known in the cricketing community when he began umpiring for his local cricket team.

Large crowds of spectators came from far and wide to view the cricket matches and the weekly newspaper *Bell's Life in Sydney and Sporting Review* remarked that the 'excitement was intense'. All classes of society came to enjoy the match and to see and be seen. The crowds dressed in their Sunday best, with everyone's attention focused on the ladies and prominent gentlemen. At a match between Braidwood and Queanbeyan on Wednesday, 16 February 1859, a new flag with 'Advance Australia' was erected and flown with great pride.

In the same year, Abraham was granted another publican licence for the Doncaster Tavern in Araluen just south of Braidwood. By 1860 he had filed for bankruptcy at the Insolvency Court. His name appeared in the newspapers of the time again and again with a list of all his assets, liabilities and debts. Just over a year later though he was granted his certificate of discharge and released from the restrictions of insolvency.

In 1862 Abraham had a strange and unwelcome guest at his house. Some young boys in the neighbourhood were out in the fields when they encountered the biggest snake they'd ever set eyes on. Stupidly, the boys began attacking the snake with sticks until they finally killed it. Excitedly, they dragged the 'monster snake' to Abraham's house. Abraham recognised the snake as a diamond python. Much to the boys' delight he measured and dissected the snake, to discover that the snake's last meal was a kangaroo rat. The snake was ten feet long.

Abraham was fifty-eight years old in 1866 but still a strong and healthy man. This was how he was described in the entrance books at Darlinghurst Gaol when he was awaiting trial for larceny. He was sentenced to four years labour with the road gangs. Sadly, the last mention of him in the records was after he had completed this sentence. He had travelled to Port Macquarie and was imprisoned for larceny again, with a sentence of four years.

Ann Moran

Ship: Hercules
Approximate age on arrival: Unknown
Crime: Unknown
Sentence: Life
Date arrived: 26 June 1802

Ann Moran was an Irish woman from Meath who was transported from Ireland towards the end of 1801. Upon arrival Ann was assigned the role of dairymaid, which was an essential role for the colony's ongoing survival. A dairymaid was required to produce milk, cheese, butter and cream for the colony. Dairy products were part of the weekly ration from the outset of the First Fleet. Being a dairymaid was a great skill to have, as there was often a surplus which they could use to earn some extra income or keep for themselves.

Dairy cows were the first type of cows to come over from England. Less than ten were sent on the First Fleet and they escaped into the bush. Over time though, the number of cattle expanded to create a healthy growing industry. Producing dairy products was generally considered a woman's occupation and was one of the more common skills cited by women in the colony. Whether they actually had experience of dairying previously, or were influenced by publications circulating in London advertising the advantages of being a dairymaid, is unknown.

Ann went to work for John Curtis not long after her arrival and a love affair developed which produced several children. Years later, in 1814, Ann and John were married in Parramatta. The next mention of Ann is on the convict muster list of 1825. Here she is listed as a widow who had earned her Ticket of Leave and was making her living as a victualler in Parramatta. There is no further mention of her.

John Lane

Ship: Camden
Approximate age on arrival: 27 years old
Crime: Robbing a counting house
Sentence: Life
Date arrived: 25 July 1831

John Lane was twenty-seven years old when he was charged with robbing a counting house. It wasn't his first offence. He had served two and a half years in Milbank prison for a prior conviction. He stood at 5 foot 4 ¾ inches tall, with brown hair and brown eyes, and had a small scar on the tip of his nose. His face was lightly freckled and he had ruddy cheeks. He had a tattoo of a ring on his right hand. John had been raised a Protestant and he could read and write.

Before his conviction, John had been living in Birmingham and had chosen the trade of making and selling umbrellas and parasols. Umbrellas were a cumbersome necessity against England's frequent miserable weather, whereas the parasol was a lightweight fashion accessory for the upper classes. Often decorated with the finest lace, ladies used their parasols in a variety of ways – to shield themselves from the sun, to stop any unwanted advances and also to flirt with. They would twirl them and peep out from under them, gracing gentlemen with coy looks. They became a very popular item for riding around town in open carriages.

By March 1831 the *Camden* was being prepared to set sail for New South Wales. John had no children to say goodbye to, but he was married to a maid named Jane Horton. Jane was distraught at the thought of being separated from her husband and feared what would become of him. She convinced herself that they must suffer the consequences of his crime together, so she secretly stowed away on the ship. Soon after the ship had left England's shores she was discovered, but did not reveal her identity or the reason for her being there for some time.

John and Jane arrived in Port Jackson in the middle of winter in 1831, however it was a mild winter compared to what they were accustomed to back home. John was facing a life sentence, but put his head down, working hard, and eight years later was awarded a Ticket of Leave. The following year though it was cancelled, as the police believed that John was mixing with prisoners at large. He was put back into the system for three months and then his Ticket of Leave was returned to him.

John worked for many years for Mr Charles Smith and was eventually awarded a Conditional Pardon in February 1845.

William Lock Thurston

Ship: Ann (2)
Approximate age on arrival: 24 years old
Crime: Horse stealing & burglary
Sentence: Death commuted to life
Date arrived: 27 February 1810

In the middle of a fiercely cold and foggy English winter, three brothers were seized for stealing horses in the Isle of Ely. William was the second child of eight children born to John Thurston and Susannah Lock. William was caught with his elder brother John and his younger brother Daniel on that winter's day. Little did they know that their actions that day would change the course of their entire family.

William stood in the docks, his hazel eyes darting anxiously around the courtroom, awaiting the fate of himself and his two brothers. When the judge read out loud their sentence to death it must have come as a brutal shock. His mother would have been distraught at the thought of losing her three eldest sons. Before the judge had left town though, a gentleman who knew William well stood up and gave him an excellent character reference and the judge was kind enough to reprieve him of his death sentence. Instead, he was sentenced to transportation for life. His brothers were not so fortunate.

While John and Daniel waited out their day of execution, their family hurriedly approached former employers and persuaded them to write glowing character references. The boys had a plan of their own though. They managed to escape from the gaol they were being held in, but were soon apprehended. Amazingly this criminal act was not held against them, as the gaol was so dilapidated it was considered an 'inducement to the attempt'. When the references were read by the judge and he considered their age and trades he soon dropped their sentence of death and commuted it to transportation for life.

The boys spent many months on a hulk named *Prudentia* until they were brought on board the ship *Ann* that was to sail them to Port Jackson. Several months into their trip their parents and younger brother Jeremiah were accused of stealing. The case was brought to trial and their father was found guilty and sentenced to transportation. Their mother Susannah and Jeremiah were both found not guilty. This was the beginning of the migration of the Thurston family. Within months of William's arrival, he was reunited with his two younger brothers Robert and Ezekiel, who were just teenagers and had arrived as convicts on the ship *Indian*. They had been charged for feloniously stealing a mare in 1809 and were both sentenced to death which was later commuted to life given their youth.

The following year they were joined by their father John, and the rest of the family saved their passage and began the arduous journey across the seas to join them. Over the course of the next ten years their wives, brothers, children and grandchildren came out and established themselves in Sydney. William's wife Mary arrived around 1815 and together they made a life for themselves. The family began working hard and buying up land in Evan which is where Penrith is today.

Together William and Mary opened up a bakery. Daniel was working as a muster clerk at the Barracks, but, unfortunately, their brother John passed away in 1816, leaving his new wife and two children behind. The family rallied around them and William and Mary took their son Dixon into their home. After William received his Conditional Pardon he and Mary left the bakery and started running a pub called the Hope & Anchor in Cambridge Street. They were able to house and employ several family members.

In 1831 William and Mary took over the Black Dog Hotel on the corner of Gloucester Street and Brown Bear Lane. It had several storeys above the pub, which included a couple of parlours and plenty of bedrooms to house his relatives. They had uninterrupted views of Circular Quay and the Hotel could be seen from the ships entering the harbour. It was frequented by sailors and other travellers, who would climb the steep hill to get to it and stagger back down bleary-eyed and worse for wear.

William and Mary's stay at the Black Dog was only short-lived. About a year or two later they passed the reins over to Emanuel Leich. Probably a wise decision, as the Black Dog's popularity and reputation grew to become one of the most notorious drinking holes in Sydney. Over the years many people died accidental deaths; they also died from the toxic brew that was served to patrons. Around this time publicans were known for 'lambing down', which was an attempt to make the grog go further by mixing it with other ingredients such as opium, cayenne pepper, tobacco and anything else they thought of. One concoction was known as 'Blow-me-skull-off' and a coroner claimed to have attended eighteen deaths relating to it and other brews served at The Black Dog.

Most of the deaths occurred when a man named Thomas G. Bolton took over. Many New Zealander Maoris and Islanders were frequenting the pub and even these stocky, well-built men were no match for the Black Dog's brew. After only a few drinks they toppled over, never to get up again. Bolton also had a pet monkey that scampered around the pub entertaining the merrymakers. It was all fun and games until the monkey attacked a young girl, leaving her face hideously scarred. The Black Dog was eventually pulled down during the outbreak of the bubonic plague in the early 1900s. The Cahill Expressway runs over its former grounds.

As for William and Mary, they retired from the innkeeper's life by moving up to Parramatta, where they lived with the family that continued to grow and support each other.

John McEntire

Ship: Alexander
Approximate age on arrival: 34 years old
Crime: Felony
Sentence: 7 years
Date arrived: 19 January 1788

The little we know about John McEntire's character comes from the journals of men who accompanied him on the First Fleet. Physically he was described by Watkin Tench, a Captain of the Marines, as an 'uncommonly robust muscular man'. He was chosen to serve out his sentence as a gamekeeper for the Governor and was entrusted with a musket, going out on many expeditions to hunt for food.

Although one of his earlier encounters with the Eora people could have gone better, he soon learned to make friends with them. He must have been fairly intelligent, as he quickly picked up their language. He possibly used their knowledge to help him learn about the animals living on the continent that were so unfamiliar to him, as well as their hunting grounds and how to identify their tracks, etc to help him provide food for the colony. The Aboriginal people were also fascinated by the white man's way of fishing and hunting, so there would have been an eager exchange of information.

George B Worgan, a surgeon, who arrived on the *Sirius*, relays in a letter to his brother, an incident in June 1788 when some Natives, or 'Children of Nature' as he describes them, approached with their dingoes. McEntire was scared that one of the dingoes was about to bite him so he quickly reacted by shooting it with his musket. The Aboriginals were so terrified of his weapon they swiftly ran away. The dingo had been shot dead.

Worgan also describes McEntire killing an Emu. He recalls the encounter with great curiosity, remarking his astonishment that the Emu could outrun their greyhound. He tells his brother Patrick that the Emu looks similar to an Ostrich and tastes like beef. He also lists the other types of birds that McEntire and the rest of the shooting party killed for food – Quails, Pigeons, Doves, Plover, Cockatoos, Parrots, Lorikeets, Crows and Hawks as well as others.

But somewhere along the line, in a matter of only two years, McEntire had become abhorred and greatly feared by the Eora people. The reason why remains a mystery. Historian Grace Karskens believes that he must have committed a serious crime such as 'violent attacks, abductions, illicit sex, theft and trespassing' to arouse such hatred. Their sudden change in attitude towards McEntire is first mentioned by Tench.

Tench makes a note in his journal that on the 7 September 1790 McEntire had accompanied Captain Nepean, Mr White and a group of men on a small expedition. They took a boat and sailed to Manly Cove with the intention of walking to Broken Bay. When they arrived they were greeted with a spectacular sight of hundreds of Aboriginal people gathered around a dead whale that had washed ashore. They were using shells tied to the end of long sticks to hack away at the dead whale's flesh. Baneelon (Bennelong) offered them great serves to take with them.

Tench describes Baneelon approaching the group with jubilation until McEntire approaches him. Baneelon had been offered some shirts as a gift and he tried to put them on to show his kin, but with difficulty. Mr White instructed McEntire to help the man, but as soon as he stepped forward Baneelon recoiled in fear and resentment. McEntire left the group so that they could carry on their exchange.

Tench also mentions another encounter between Baneelon and McEntire when Baneelon came to visit the Governor's residence in October 1790. Baneelon was running through the house, greeting the staff and other visitors with joy, kissing some of them on the cheeks. When he saw McEntire his whole demeanour changed dramatically and he would not let McEntire near him.

Whatever McEntire had done to cause such a reaction from Baneelon had finally caught up with him. In December that year, he and two other gamekeepers went on a hunting expedition when they were approached by several Aborigines with spears. McEntire immediately put down his gun and told the others, 'Don't be afraid, I know them'. He stepped forward and greeted them in their own language. During their conversation one of the Aboriginal men stepped up onto a fallen tree and, without hesitation, threw his spear, which lodged into McEntire's side. McEntire cried out, 'I'm a dead man', and the Aboriginal group fled.

One of his companions broke off the end of the spear and the other began to chase after the offender but soon retreated as they were just too fast. McEntire insisted on trying to get back to town as he did not want to die in the bush. The three men struggled to make it back, with McEntire losing a large amount of blood in the process. Their movements were slow but they eventually arrived about two o'clock in the morning.

When a doctor examined him it was confirmed that it was unlikely that he would survive the wound. Surgeons argued back and forth over whether or not to pull the spear out. At first they thought better of it, but as time passed they decided to pull it out. McEntire lingered for days and as he did he confessed to all manner of crimes. When asked about his treatment of the Aboriginals he only confessed to having injured one. Tench comments on this, stating that many did not believe him, judging from what they knew to be 'his general character and other circumstances'.

On 20 January 1791, John McEntire died. It had been eight days since they had pulled the spear out. The man who speared McEntire with a woomera was a well-known Aboriginal by the name of Pemulwuy. His death enraged Governor Phillip who sent out a party to kill Pemulwuy, but they came back unsuccessful in their mission. What happened between him and the Eora people remains a mystery.

Francis Ambrose

Ship: Bussorah Merchant
Approximate age on arrival: 15 years old
Crime: Stealing a handkerchief
Sentence: 14 years
Date arrived: 26 July 1828

It was going on dusk when a stage coach rattled its way through the cobbled streets of central London carrying three gentlemen. Francis Ambrose a young lad of just fourteen years skittered after the coach, his red hair flapping in the breeze. As the coach slowed to take the corner at Church Lane, Whitechapel, Francis seized his opportunity and quietly leapt onto the back of the coach. With one hand holding him steady he reached with his other hand, delving into the pocket of an unsuspecting passenger and pulling out the gentleman's handkerchief. Happy with his booty, he then swiftly stepped off the coach.

Unfortunately for Francis the entire exchange, so gracefully executed, was witnessed by a police officer. As Francis casually began to saunter away the officer placed a heavy hand on his shoulder. When the officer frisked him he found 6s. 3d in his pocket. In a thick Irish accent Francis said to the officer, 'You may take that, and let me go', but the officer refused. A week later, when Francis had his day in court, he was found guilty and sentenced to transportation for fourteen years.

Nearly four months later Francis boarded the *Bussorah Merchant* convict ship bound for New South Wales. Convicts were treated quite well on board. They were allowed up on deck to bask in the sunshine whenever the weather permitted. However, early on in the journey it became apparent that a crew member had smallpox. Because of this, when the vessel arrived at Port Jackson in July it was turned away and quarantined in Spring Cove, Manly.

This marked the beginning of the use of North Head as the quarantine area for incoming ships.

A few months prior to the arrival of the *Bussorah Merchant* Governor Darling's son Edward had died from whooping cough, which was brought to New South Wales on board the *Morley*. The following year the need for a quarantine station was reinforced when a cholera pandemic spread throughout Europe. Governor Darling created the Quarantine Act of 1832. The Quarantine Station at Manly is still standing today and offers visitors a rich history and insight into early Australian medical treatments and the diseases brought by the incoming ships.

Francis spent seven long weeks in Spring Cove. Thankfully there were no further outbreaks of smallpox. On 15 September, at the end of their detention, a convict muster was held and the details of each convict were recorded. Francis' dark red hair and hazel eyes were noted, along with the scars on his arms, the wart on his knuckle and his pock-pitted scarred face. He was assigned to work for a lady named Mary, but this assignment didn't last long as the following year he was caught stealing again and sent to a penal settlement for three years.

When Francis returned to Sydney he was in his twenties, but had not matured in any way as he was regularly in and out of trouble. He ran away many times, missed compulsory attendance at chapel, was caught in a drunken state at work and even assaulted a constable. For these crimes he received lashes with the cat-o-nine tails and work assignments with the iron gangs. After 1837 he disappears from the record.

Catherine Harvey

Ship: Minstrel
Approximate age on arrival: 46 years old
Crime: Stealing beef
Sentence: Life
Date arrived: 25 October 1812

In 1793 Catherine Harvey stood hand in hand in the All Hallows church in London with her soon to be husband Benjamin Goddard. From the outside, the church was unassuming — a simple design tucked inside an ancient Roman wall that once wrapped around the heart of London. Inside the church, which is still around today, stand fluted Ionic columns in a beautiful space that is bathed in natural light from the high windows. It was here that Catherine and Benjamin looked into each other's eyes and exchanged their wedding vows.

Over the next few years Catherine and Benjamin expanded their family to six. The early years of their marriage were a difficult time for many in Britain; expansion had led to an increase in bread prices and the poorer classes were feeling the pinch. Benjamin had a job as a watchmaker but Catherine, being saddled with so many small children, was unable to work much. When she could, she worked as a silk-winder which was fiddly work that required a great deal of patience; she would take the silk from cocoons and thread them around spindles. The couple never had quite enough money coming in and Catherine in her desperation turned to crime in order to feed her family.

Her first brush with the law was in 1803 when she found herself caught up in a robbery with her friend Ann Price. On 17 November the two women, along with a young man, were seen loitering a few doors up from a shop which sold printed cotton. Moments later Ann and the man entered the shop and purchased some cotton. They told the shopkeeper that they would be back the following day to purchase other prints. Five minutes after their arrival Catherine wandered into the shop and also purchased some cotton. The three left together, however, Ann and the man headed up North Street and Catherine went the other way. It was then that the shop owner noticed some of her merchandise missing and followed Ann and the man. She casually called out to Ann on the pretence of needing more information regarding her order. Ann stopped, but the man continued walking. After talking to her for a while about her purchase she saw Ann trying to conceal the stolen cotton in her hand. Ann was seized and the police were called. The shopkeeper was convinced Catherine had been in on it too.

Both Catherine and Ann were thrown in Newgate Prison to await their trial. The women endured thirteen long days in Newgate, which was overrun with vermin, disease and lice and the smell was an overwhelming assault on the senses. The guards were known to be particularly cruel, chaining some inmates to the walls and extorting money from them for even the smallest of privileges such as food and bedding. Catherine and Ann would have regularly heard the sounds of growing crowds gathering outside around the gallows awaiting the next execution.

The trial took place two weeks later on 30 November. After hearing the shopkeeper's and police account of what they had witnessed it was Ann's turn to speak and defend herself. She cried, *"I throw myself on the mercy of the Court; it was poverty that drove me to it; the other woman knows nothing about it."* The judge handed down a verdict of not guilty for Catherine, but Ann was found guilty and sentenced to the House of Corrections for twelve months, with a fine of 1 shilling. Catherine was released and returned to her family.

Years passed and their situation had not improved. Catherine turned to crime again, risking more time in Newgate and possible death if caught. Out of complete and utter desperation she entered a butcher's in Whitechapel dressed in an oversized cloak which she used to conceal eleven pounds of beef. The owner John Luckit had been watching her closely and confronted her. She dropped the beef and begged for his mercy. Unfortunately, he alerted the police and she was again sent to

Newgate. In court, on the 18 September 1811, she pleaded to the judge, *"I have got a small family of four children, none of them earn any thing."* Much to her family's relief the judge took pity on her and found her guilty but only fined her 1 shilling and discharged her.

Sadly, only three months later she found herself in the same predicament. This time she had stolen 17 pairs of stockings and the judge did not go easy on her. She was found guilty and sentenced to death. Thankfully her sentence was later commuted to transportation for life. Catherine spent six long months in Newgate prison trying to get used to the idea of being transported to the other side of the world. Unable to bear the thought of being separated from her family she made an appeal to take one of her children with her, which was granted. So, on 4 June 1812, exactly six months from the day of her trial, she and her son Benjamin set sail on board the *Minstrel* to New South Wales. Benjamin was roughly eleven years of age.

The voyage was fairly uneventful. The ship carried 127 female convicts and there were only two deaths during the trip. They sailed alongside the *Indefatigable* for most of the way. Little Benjamin was probably doted on by the women. When they arrived in Port Jackson 143 days later, *The Sydney Gazette and NSW Advertiser* reported that the women were all in a healthy state. Indents were written up, they were given clothing or 'slops', and most of the women were put on a boat a few days later and sailed to the Female Factory in Parramatta. Three weeks after their arrival they experienced their first big storm. The torrential rain bucketed down giant hail that destroyed crops and even killed some smaller livestock. The women were lucky that the storm hit while they were on land and not at sea.

Back home Catherine's husband was busy applying for passage to join them. Convicts could apply to have their significant other sent out to New South Wales at the government's expense. This privilege was usually granted to men for their wives to join them in order to balance out the very uneven numbers between the sexes in the hope of bringing some morality to the colony. It was also a way of relieving the pressure on the stores, as they would only allow partners to come over who could prove that they could support themselves and their convict spouses. The last thing they needed was more mouths to feed. The convicts who applied usually did so after displaying several years of good behaviour.

Although Benjamin's application was not granted, he managed to convince the powers that be to let him work for his passage, and that of his daughter Susannah's, on board the ship. The two left England on 3 December 1812 and arrived 11 June 1813. A few weeks after their arrival Catherine was granted her Ticket of Leave and struck off the victualling list. This was quite extraordinary for a lifer to receive a Ticket of Leave so quickly. It shows the advantage for women entering the matrimonial state. Catherine was able to look after her family and help her husband with his watchmaking business and the government had two less mouths to feed.

Years later the family were granted land and set up a home in Windsor. Originally named 'Green

Hills' due to its lush vegetation and rich soil, Windsor is a picturesque town on the banks of the Hawkesbury River. In the very early days of colonisation Windsor produced roughly half of the food supply for Sydney. A boat travelled down the Hawkesbury River and onto Sydney Harbour to deliver the produce to the main centre. The years of poverty and deprivation in England were over. The desperate act of stealing eleven pounds of beef from a butcher to feed her family no longer necessary, Catherine could now give thanks for the abundance around her as her family grew and prospered.

Over the years their children married, and it wasn't long before Catherine and Benjamin welcomed grandchildren into the fold. Catherine died in 1840 having reached her seventies.

Frederick Brook Carrick

Ship: Glory
Approximate age on arrival: 23 years old
Crime: Stealing
Sentence: Death commuted to life
Date arrived: 14 September 1818

Frederick was a young lad living in England and completing an apprenticeship in cabinetmaking when he met the love of his life Sarah Atkins. The two quickly fell in love and wanted nothing more than to marry and have children. When Sarah discovered she was pregnant Frederick told his father that he intended to marry her. His father, Thomas, forbade the match, but Frederick was determined to marry Sarah even if it meant defying his father, so Thomas put an advertisement in the paper forbidding the marriage and cautioning clergymen not to solemnize the union. However, months later in a Parish in Lechlade in the county of Gloucester they found a clergyman willing to help them. On 5 September 1814 the two exchanged their vows and became man and wife.

A few months later they welcomed the birth of their first child, who they named Frederick Adolphus Carrick, and in 1816 gave him a little sister named Henrietta. They were a happy unit until the following year, when Frederick was accused of stealing a bank note belonging to Reverend John D'Arcy Preston. The reverend had put the bank note in his desk drawer at Corpis Christi College in Oxford and a witness claimed to have seen Frederick carrying the desk through the courtyard of the college. Frederick was apprehended but pleaded his innocence. When the case was heard he was found not guilty and returned to his family.

Tragically, not long after his brush with the law Frederick's infant daughter Henrietta died. Before his baby was even buried he had been arrested again. This time he was accused of stealing a box of valuables belonging to his landlord John Churchman. Inside the box were 2 strings of beads, 3 gold rings, a locket, a brooch, 2 seals and some money. Churchman realised the box was missing after Frederick had left for the day and alerted the police. The police apprehended Frederick, and frisked him, but came up empty-handed. Much to the annoyance and frustration of Churchman, the police had no choice but to release Frederick. Convinced of his guilt, Churchman followed Frederick's movements all day and watched him enter a pawnbroker's and sell the brooch. With a pocket full of money and a smile on his face, Frederick turned to leave the shop only to be seized by Churchman. He was then dragged to Bow Street Police Station, where he was arrested. Frederick was later found guilty and sentenced to death.

Frederick was returned to Newgate Prison after his trial and there he stayed until his sentence was commuted to transportation for life. He was then transferred to a prison hulk called the *Bellerophon,* which was moored in Woolwich, to await a ship to take him to New South Wales. Three months later Frederick bid his family farewell and boarded the ship *Glory* at Sheerness along with fellow convict Israel Chapman. The journey took roughly six months. When they arrived at Port Jackson, Frederick's details were noted on his indent. He was 5 foot 11 inches tall with dark brown hair and hazel eyes.

Over the next few years Frederick doggedly served out his sentence and endured a life without his wife and son. The hope of reuniting with them one day pushed him to go on. Five years later his dream was realised when Sarah and little Frederick arrived in the colony after travelling on the *Jupiter*. Frederick barely recognised his son who was now 11 years of age. After an emotional reunion, Frederick moved his wife and son into his residence with his employer John Ellis in Kent Street.

Sarah and Frederick wasted no time expanding their family, first with the birth of their daughter Selina, followed by Henry, and lastly Thomas. With so many mouths to feed they realised that they needed a steady, reliable income, so Frederick supported his growing family by starting up a new business in George Street as a house and ship joiner. Sarah too contributed by starting her own business selling baked goods, fruit and confectionery. Sadly, Thomas died the following year in 1828.

Frederick and Sarah spend the next five years happily raising their family and working hard at their businesses. Frederick earned himself a Ticket of Leave allowing him to remain and work in Sydney and the couple used their hard-earned savings to take over the running of the Golden Anchor Tavern in Bridge Street. Sadly, their first son Frederick Adolphus' health begins to deteriorate. The couple tend to their son as he suffers from a painful and lingering illness, but it eventually takes his life at the age of twenty. His death is a devasting blow to their close-knit family. This is the third child that Frederick and Sarah have lost.

Two years later Frederick and Sarah use their savings to purchase land on the north side of Bridge Street for a total of 200 pounds and 5 shillings. Frederick is frequently in the newspapers chasing his customers to settle their debts with him. He ends up taking over another pub called the Oxford Arms in Sydney. In May the following year Frederick finally receives his Absolute Pardon declaring him to be a free man. He and his family have come so far from the days when he was arrested and sentenced to death. He has matured into a successful, hard-working man, dedicated to his family, and a well-respected member of the community. So, when a man by the name of Russell tries to damage this hard-earned reputation, Frederick puts up a fight.

Robert Russell was an ironmonger living in the same street as the Carrick family. Whilst Frederick was visiting England, something he couldn't do until he had earned his Absolute Pardon, Russell began courting his daughter Selina. Selina was only fifteen years old at the time. Russell was about thirty and visited Selina frequently with her mother's consent. Ten months later, when Selina went to Maitland to visit a friend, she discovered she was pregnant with his child. Selina immediately wrote to Russell informing him of the news and her desire for him to marry her. He wrote back professing his love for her and reassuring her by promising to come to Maitland in three weeks' time and marry her. He signed off *"Your much attached and honorable Robert"*.

Three weeks passed and there was no sign of Robert. Selina heard that Russell had married another woman. The broken-hearted Selina fell very ill with the news and it took her a month to be well enough to travel back home to Sydney. Once there she was prematurely confined due to her health. She delivered the baby in December, a beautiful baby boy which she named Arthur Henry Carrick, but he only lived a few months.

To save face, Russell spread rumours defaming Selina and her parents. The whole situation and Russell's ongoing slander had sullied the Carrick name and left his daughter devastated and humiliated. In the eyes of the community she was seen as compromised and her future prospects were greatly damaged. Frederick was furious. He wanted retribution, so took Russell to court, suing him for £2,000 for damages of the loss of Selina's help in running his household affairs for the time she was pregnant and for the injury to their character. Russell pleaded not guilty. Russell's defence was that after sending the letter with promises to marry her he learned that she was an 'abandoned and profligate strumpet'. He asserted that he was the victim having been being seduced, not the seducer. The jury retired for only twenty minutes and came back with a verdict for the plaintiff awarding Carrick £300 in compensation.

Selina did get her happy ending. Around the time of the trial she met another man named Isiah Hurst who asked her to marry him. She accepted and the couple wed in Sydney that year. They moved to Tasmania and had many children together.

In February 1844 Frederick died aged 48. He was buried at Rookwood Cemetery.

Isaac Crane

Ship: Surrey
Approximate age on arrival: 24 years old
Crime: Receiving stolen goods
Sentence: 7 years
Date arrived: 28 July 1814

At midday on Saturday, 25 January 1812 the clickety-clack of Isaac Crane's horse and cart could be heard meandering its way down the cobbled streets of Clerkenwell, London. As Isaac loped around the bend into Smith Street he spotted Thomas Dutton and pulled up his horse alongside his cart. Thomas greeted Isaac and hurriedly shifted four bags of oats from his cart onto Isaac's. Isaac then covered the oats with an empty sack and made haste up Goswell Road. The entire exchange was witnessed by an onlooker who thought it was suspicious behaviour and reported it to the authorities.

Both men were arrested for theft and sent to court.

When the case was heard, the court learned that Thomas had been sent by his employer Mr Willan, to pick up several bags of oats and take them to feed his horses. The delivery was four bags short when it arrived. Thomas Dutton was found guilty of stealing and sentenced to confinement for two years in the House of Corrections and fined one shilling. Isaac was found not guilty.

More than six months later, thinking that he had got away with it, Isaac was again arrested for the crime. A servant of Mr Willan's named Henry Bellas had found the missing bags of oats in Isaac's stable. The officer who arrested Isaac accosted him as he left the Bedford Arms late one evening. Isaac struggled to get free but the officer managed to overpower him. This time he was found guilty of receiving stolen goods and sentenced to transportation for seven years.

After the trial Isaac was sent to a prison hulk moored in Portsmouth to await a ship to take him to New Holland. It wasn't until February

1814 that he boarded the *Surrey* and began his journey to New South Wales. The voyage was horrendous as there was an outbreak of Typhus that spread rapidly among the prisoners and crew. Typhus was a terrible disease that started with splitting headaches, then severe fevers followed by abdominal pains, diarrhea and vomiting and a nasty rash. Internal organs would swell and then the person died. The Captain ordered that the ship be regularly cleaned and fumigated to try and quell the spread of disease. Despite these efforts people continued to be infected and died.

As they neared Port Jackson the Captain had taken with fever and many of the crew were dead or dying. Fortunately, another ship called the *Broxbornebury* came by. A volunteer from that ship came aboard and assisted them into the harbour. By the time they reached Port Jackson a total of 36 convicts had died along with the master and 14 other crew members. The ship was immediately put into quarantine until there were no further signs of the disease.

Before Isaac left isolation, his convict indent was written up. Isaac was reported to be 5 foot 5 1/2 inches tall with dark eyes and black hair. He told the clerk that he was originally from Camden Town, London, where he had worked as a bricklayer. He was then issued with slops and sent on to Windsor to work the remainder of his sentence. Isaac was assigned to Thomas White Winder, a merchant and farmer who came free to New South Wales on the *Frederick*. Isaac kept out of trouble, working hard and earned himself a Ticket of Leave.

In 1822 Isaac married Elizabeth Duncan. Elizabeth had been sent to New South Wales as a convict on board the *Morley* in 1820. She had light brown hair and blue eyes, with a fair but ruddy complexion. Elizabeth had been sentenced to fourteen years transportation for forging bank notes. After the wedding she was assigned to her husband. She quickly fell pregnant and the following year they welcomed their daughter Ann into the world. In 1825 Elizabeth gave her a little brother, who they named William Alexander. Both children were baptised at St Philips church in Sydney, which still stands today.

However, somewhere along the way their marriage unravelled, and Elizabeth found love with another man named Michael Cohen. One newspaper described him as "a well-dressed, well-fed, buckram-starched, and bang-up swell." In 1839 Elizabeth bigamously married Michael in Richmond. For many years they lived and worked together at the Forbes Hotel without the community realising that she was also still married to Isaac. Isaac and Elizabeth must have continued to have a friendship as he never went to the authorities to inform them that she was still married to him. But no one can keep a secret long in a small town and rumours began to circulate. Eventually the gossip caught the ear of the local Pastor of St Peters church, who considered it his moral duty to speak up. The scandal rocked the community and the oncoming court case was eagerly anticipated and a great source of entertainment.

Isaac, Elizabeth and Michael were all brought before the courts in March 1843. A copy of the first marriage certificate was produced and the clergymen who married them were both called as witnesses. To the utter astonishment of the eagerly awaiting crowd gathered in the courtroom the case was dismissed! Elizabeth walked out with her two husbands in tow.

Isaac Crane spent the rest of his life in Windsor. One evening he went and sat on his verandah and admired his view. He settled in, enjoying the sounds of the bush and birds and as the sun slowly made its way down he drifted off to sleep. He never woke up. He was roughly 65 years old when the cold night took him peacefully.

Glossary

Absolute Pardon – A highly sought after piece of paper that restored a convict's freedom. They were given all their citizenship rights and allowed to leave the colony. They were permitted to return to the British Isles if they so chose. The first Absolute Pardon was issued in 1790 to a convict named John Irving.

Bagatelle – A very similar game to billiards but uses the addition of wooden pegs to obstruct the ball from going into the holes. It was introduced to Britain in the early 1800s.

Broad arrow – A symbol stamped onto an object or piece of clothing that identified it as belonging to the government.

Certificate of Freedom – This was awarded to a convict when they had completed their sentence. It was issued for the first time in 1810 in NSW.

When a convict's sentence was complete they applied to a magistrate who checked their ship indent and issued the certificate when satisfied that the sentence had expired.

Conditional Pardon – This was awarded to convicts who had been given a life sentence. It released them from being a prisoner but all their rights were not restored. They were unable to leave the colony and return to the British Isles.

Coopering – The traditional craft of making wooden barrels and buckets.

Holey dollar and dump – The middle of a Spanish coin was punched out to create two coins. The 'dump' was the middle section and was worth fifteen pence and the 'holey dollar' was worth five shillings.

Hominy – Plain porridge, made from maize that had been ground down by convicts serving out their punishment on the treadmill. It was served to convicts for breakfast.

King's Stores – The government supplies of food, clothing, tools and equipment etc. that were stored and rationed out for the convicts and settlers when in need.

Lifers – Early slang for convicts serving a life sentence.

Magpie – A black and bright yellow uniform given to convicts as a form of punishment. It was fashioned to induce shame and was often issued to absconders so they could be clearly seen.

Oakum – Tarred fibre used for sealing gaps.

Orlop – The lowest deck of a wooden sailing ship with three or more decks. It sat below water level.

Privies – A privy was a toilet located in a shed away from the main house.

Slops – Cheaply made, loose clothing.

Spanker boom – A spanker is a sail on a ship and a boom is the pole it attaches to.

Tank Stream – A freshwater stream running through to Sydney Cove and used by the early settlers. It got its name from the series of tanks cut into the sandstone next to the stream. It fell out of use in 1826.

Ticket of Leave – Issued to convicts for good behaviour. It allowed a convict to work for themselves but they were not to leave a specified area. They had to have their certificate on them at all times.

Ticketers – Early slang for a man or woman holding a Ticket of Leave.

Victualler – A person holding a licence to sell alcohol.

Victualling List – A list of people who depend on the government's food stores.

Watchhouse – A short-term holding place for convicts who have been arrested or are awaiting trial.

Woomera – An Aboriginal throwing stick.

Bibliography

James Milward
- "Derbyshire Lent Assizes" *Derby Mercury*, April 1, 1829
- Australian Convict Transportation Registers – Other Fleets & Ships, 1791-1868
- NSW, Convict Indents, 1788-1842
- NSW, Australia, Convict Records, 1810-1891 Cockatoo Island: Index to Convicts, 1833-1834
- March 1836 New South Wales, Australia, Tickets of Leave, 1810-1869
- NSW and Tasmania, Australia, Convict Pardons and Tickets of Leave, 1834-1859 1834 – 1838
- Dictionary of Sydney. *Cockatoo Island*. Last modified April 23, 2014. http://home.dictionaryofsydney.org/cockatoo-island/
- Chambers, M. (2000). *Cockatoo Island Dockyard, a Guide to the Records*. National Archives of Australia.

- Laugesen, A. (2002). *Convict words, language in early colonial Australia.* Oxford University Press
- National Library of Australia. *Tickets of Leave/ Certificates of Freedom/ Pardons.* https://www.nla.gov.au/research-guides/convicts/tickets-of-leave
- Petersen, J. (2003, reprinted with corrections 2006)*Hyde Park Barracks Museum Guidebook,* Historic Houses Trust
- "Charge of Murder." *The Sydney Morning Herald*, June 2, 1845
- "*Domestic Intelligence.*" *The Sydney Morning Herald*, June 3, 1845
- "Inquests." *The Australian*, June 5, 1845
- *Instructions for the guidance of the superintendent and Subordinate Offices of the Establishment of Convicts in Hyde Park Barracks,* Sydney 1825.

Tom Tough
- *UK, Prison Hulk Registers and Letter Books, 1802-1849 (October 25, 1838)*
- New South Wales, Australia, Convict Indents, 1788-1842 (April 1, 1834)
- NSW, Australia, Gaol Description and Entrance Books, Darlinghurst 1818 – 1930 (1840)

- NSW, Australia, Gaol Description and Entrance Books, Darlinghurst 1818 – 1930, (1841)
- NSW, Australia, Gaol Description and Entrance Books, 1818 – 1930 (November 23, 1841)
- "Domestic Intelligence." *The Sydney Herald*, January 29, 1842
- New South Wales, Australia, Tickets of Leave, 1810-1869, (January 25, 1844)
- Petersen, J. (2003, reprinted with corrections 2006)*Hyde Park Barracks Museum Guidebook*, Historic Houses Trust
- New South Wales, Australia, Registers of Convicts' Applications to Marry, 1826-1851(February 5, 1844)
- New South Wales, Australia, Registers of Convicts' Applications to Marry, 1826-1851 (May 13, 1846)
- NSW and Tasmania, Australia Convict Musters, Tasmania, 1846
- NSW, Australia, Registers of Convicts Applications to Marry, Refused 1847
- "Family Notices." *The Sydney Morning Herald*, January 18, 1848
- "Family Notices." *The Maitland Mercury & Hunter River General Advertiser*, January 22, 1848

- NSW, Australia, Convict Registers of Conditional and Absolute Pardons, Conditional, 1848
- "Advertising." *The Sydney Morning Herald*, March 8, 1853
- "The Police Register." *Bell's Life in Sydney and Sporting Reviewer*, June 25, 1853
- "Advertising." *The Sydney Morning Herald*, July 19, 1853
- NSW, Australia, Gaol Description and Entrance Books, 1818 – 1930 (Entrance Book, Darlinghurst 1853)
- NSW, Australia, Gaol Description and Entrance Books, 1818 – 1930 (Entrance Book, Darlinghurst 1853)
- "Advertising." *The Sydney Morning Herald*, January 24, 1854
- *Empire*, October 3, 1854
- "Central Police Court. Tuesday." *The Sydney Morning Herald*, October 4, 1854
- "Sydney Police Court. Tuesday." *Empire*, October 4, 1854
- "Extensive Robbery of Jewellery." *The Argus*, October 4, 1854
- "Sydney Quarter Sessions. Thursday." *The Sydney Morning Herald*, November 17, 1854
- NSW, Australia, Criminal Court Records, 1830 – 1845 (November 17, 1854)

- NSW, Australia, Gaol Description and Entrance Books, 1818 – 1930 (March 18, 1858)
- New South Wales, Australia, Gaol Description and Entrance Books, 1818-1930 (1867)

Elizabeth Sullivan
- NSW, Australia, Tickets of Leave, 1824 – 1867 (1833)
- *Old Bailey Proceedings Online* (www.oldbaileyonline.org, version 7.2, 13 February 2018), February 1836 (t18360229).
- NSW, Australia, Convict Indents, 1788 – 1842 (1836)
- NSW, Australia, Registers of Convicts' Applications to Marry, 1826 – 1851
- Australia, Marriage Index, 1788 – 1950
- 1841 NSW, Australia, Census
- NSW, Australia, Certificates of Freedom, 1810 – 1814, 1827 – 1867 (July 1843)
- "Challenges – Man, Woman, Dog, and Cock." *Bell's Life in Sydney and Sporting Reviewer*, September 13, 1845
- "Foul Tongue V. Dirty Linen." *Bells Life in Sydney and Sporting Reviewer*, August 7, 1847
- "The Heroine of Cooks River." *Bells Life in Sydney and Sporting Reviewer* , October 8, 1853

- Daniels, K. (1998). *Convict Women*, St Leonards, NSW, Allen & Unwin.
- Maynard, M. *Australian Dress*. Love to Know, Beauty & Fashion *https://fashion-history.lovetoknow.com/clothing-around-world/australian-dress*. Visited: June 13, 2018.

Ann Armsden
- Cobley, J. (1989). *The Crimes of the Lady Juliana Convicts – 1790*, Library of Australian History Sydney
- Flynn, M. (2001). *The Second Fleet, Britain's Grim Convict Armada of 1790*, Library of Australian History, Sydney
- Karskens, G. (1999). *Inside the Rocks, the Archaeology of a Neighbourhood*, Hale & Iremonger Pty Ltd
- Rees, S. (2002). *The Floating Brothel*, Hodder Headline Australia Pty Limited
- NSW, Australia, Settler and Convict Lists, 1787
- Australian Convict Transportation Registers – First Fleet
- NSW and Tasmania, Australia Convict Musters, 1806
- "Sydney." *The Sydney Gazette and NSW Advertiser*, June 14, 1807

- "London." *The Sydney Gazette and NSW Advertiser*, June 21, 1807
- "Sydney." *The Sydney Gazette and NSW Advertiser*, July 19, 1807
- "Sydney." *The Sydney Gazette and NSW Advertiser*, July 26, 1807
- "Classified Advertising." *The Sydney Gazette and NSW Advertiser*, March 26, 1809
- Australia, Marriage Index, 1810
- NSW and Tasmania, Australia Convict Musters 1811
- NSW, Australia, Colonial Secretary's Papers 1822

Frederick Mitton

- NSW, Australia, Convict Indents, Non-Annotated Printed Indents, 1840 – 1842.
- List of Convict with Particulars, 1840
- Witton, V. *Damming the Cooks River*, Dictionary of Sydney, 2013, <u>http://dictionaryofsydney.org/entry/damming_the_cooks_river</u>. *Viewed: February 15, 2018*
- "News of the day, Piracy." *The Sydney Monitor*, April 20, 1840.
- "Attempted Escape from the Cooks River Gang." *The Sydney Gazette and NSW Advertiser*, April 21, 1840.

- "Sydney Quarter Sessions." *The Australian,* May 28 1840.
- *NSW, Australian, Gaol Description & Entrance Books, Sydney, 1840*
- Barry. J V, "Maconochie, Alexander (1787–1860)", *Australian Dictionary of Biography*, National Centre of Biography, Australian National University, http://adb.anu.edu.au/biography/maconochie-alexander-2417/text3207, viewed 15 February 2018.
- *NSW, Australian, Gaol Description & Entrance Books, Darlinghurst NSW, 1847.*
- "Law Intelligence. Central Criminal Court. Monday". *The Sydney Morning Herald,* August 24, 1847.
- "Central Criminal Court – Monday. Before his Honor Mr Justice Dickinson. Uttering a Forged Cheque" *Sydney Chronicle,* August 25, 1847
- "Central Criminal Court". *Bell's Life in Sydney and Sporting Reviewer,* August 28 1847
- "Law Intelligence. Central Criminal Sessions". *The Sydney Morning Herald,* August 30, 1847.
- NSW, Australia, Tickets of Leave, October 17, 1850

John Dwyer
- NSW, Australia, Convict Indents, 1830-1832
- NSW, Australia, Settler and Convict Lists, 1828 – 1832
- NSW, Australia, Convict Indents, Annotated Printed Indentures, 1832
- NSW, Australia, Settler and Convict Lists, 1787 – 1834
- (2004). *Index to convict deaths found in Port Macquarie from 'The Winding Sheet'*. Port Macquarie Historic Society
- "Classified Advertising." *The Sydney Gazette and NSW Advertiser*, March 28, 1833
- "Classified Advertising." *The Sydney Gazette and NSW Advertiser*, April 11, 1833
- "Classified Advertising." *The Sydney Gazette and NSW Advertiser*, May 2, 1833
- Rogers, F. (ed.), (1982). *Port Macquarie, a History to 1850.* Hastings District Historical Society
- Australian Death Index, 1836
- NSW, Australia, Convict Death Register

James Frazer
- *Old Bailey Proceedings Online* (www.oldbaileyonline.org, version 8.0, 16 March 2018), April 1826 (18260406).

- Australian Joint Copying Project, State library of Qld, Microfilm Roll 88, Class and piece number HO11/6, Page number 79 (41)
- *NSW, Australia, Convict Indents, Bound Indentures, 1827*
- *NSW Australia, Registers of Convicts Application to Marry, 1826 – 1851*
- *Australian Marriage Index, 1788 – 1950*
- "Domestic Intelligence." *The Sydney Monitor*, December 7, 1831
- "Domestic Intelligence." *The Sydney Herald*, December 19, 1831
- *NSW, Australia, Gaol Description and Entrance Books, Sydney, 1831*
- "Domestic Intelligence." *The Sydney Monitor*, February 27, 1833
- "Police Report." *The Sydney Gazette and NSW Advertiser*, February 28, 1833
- Australian Joint Copying Project, State library of Qld, Microfilm Roll 90, Class and piece number HO11/9, Page number 243 (123)
- "Quarter Sessions." *The Sydney Monitor*, December 28, 1833
- *NSW, Australia, Convict Indents, Annotated Printed Indentures, 1834*
- *NSW, Australia, Settler and Convict Lists, Convicts arrived, 1833 – 1834*

- "Ship News." *The Sydney Gazette and NSW Advertiser*, November 1, 1836
- "Creditors of James Frazer." *The Sydney Gazette and NSW Advertiser*, November 12, 1836
- NSW, Australia, Tickets of Leave, March 1842
- NSW and Tasmania, Australia, Convict Pardons and Tickets of Leave, (Pardons)
- NSW National Parks and Wildlife Services. *Goat Island*. Visited March 17, 2018. https://www.nationalparks.nsw.gov.au/things-to-do/historic-buildings-places/goat-island

Robert Hudson
- "Cutting and Stabbing." Bell's Weekly Messenger , April 3, 1836
- NSW, Australia, Convict Indents, Annotated Printed Indentures, 1837
- Convict Muster 1837
- Sydney living Museums. *What was the 'Rum' hospital?*, https://sydneylivingmuseums.com.au/what-was-rum-hospital. Visited: April, 6 2018.
- Camden History Notes. *Convalescent hospital follows Florence Nightingale,* Last modified January 28, 2018. https://camdenhistorynotes.wordpress.com/2018/01/25/carrington-hospital-camden/

- NSW, Australia, Gaol Description and Entrance Books, Darlinghurst, 1841
- "The Macquarie Street Murder." *The Sydney Herald*, September 21, 1841
- "The Late Atrocious Murder at the General Hospital." *The Sydney Gazette and NSW Advertiser*, September 21, 1841
- "Coroner's Inquest – Wilful Murder." *Australasian Chronicle*, Tuesday 21 September
- "The Murder in Macquarie Street." *The Sydney Monitor and Commercial Advertiser*, September 22, 1841
- *NSW, Australia, Gaol Description and Entrance Books, Darlinghurst, 1841*
- "Law Intelligence." *The Sydney Herald*, October 15, 1841
- "Law Intelligence." *The Sydney Gazette and NSW Advertiser*, October 16, 1841
- "Thursday, October 14." *Australasian Chronicle*, October 16 1841
- "Domestic Intelligence." *The Sydney Herald*, October 30, 1841

George Vigers
- Australian Convict Transportation Registers – Other Fleets & Ships, 1826
- NSW, Australia, Convict Indents, 1827 – 1828

- NSW, Australia Convict Ship Muster Rolls and Related Records, 1828
- NSW, Australia, Gaol Description and Entrance Books, April 21, 1828
- NSW, Australia, Gaol Description and Entrance Books, July 4, 1828
- NSW, Australia Census, 1828
- NSW, Australia, Gaol Description and Entrance Books, January 19, 1829
- NSW, Australia, Gaol Description and Entrance Books, June 22, 1829
- NSW, Australia, Gaol Description and Entrance Books, September 17, 1829
- NSW, Australia, Gaol Description and Entrance Books, November 23, 1829
- "Advertiser." *The Sydney Gazette and NSW Advertiser*, December 1, 1829
- NSW, Australia, Gaol Description and Entrance Books, Parramatta, May 21, 1831
- NSW, Australia, Gaol Description and Entrance Books, Parramatta, July 27, 1831
- "Advertiser." *The Sydney Gazette and NSW Advertiser*, October 27, 1831 - November 10, 1831
- NSW, Australia, Gaol Description and Entrance Books, February 1, 1832
- "Classified Advertising." *The Sydney Gazette and NSW Advertiser*, February 2 – 16, 1832

- "Classified Advertising." *The Sydney Gazette and NSW Advertiser*, March 8, 1832
- "Sydney Gazette. Saturday, August 23, 1834." *The Sydney Gazette and NSW Advertiser*, August 23, 1834
- NSW, Australia, Gaol Description and Entrance Books, November 21, 1839
- NSW, Australia, Gaol Description and Entrance Books, April 25, 1840
- Supreme Criminal Court. Wednesday. *The Australian*, May 9, 1840
- Law Intelligence. Supreme Court – Criminal Side. *The Sydney Herald*, May 13, 1840
- NSW, Australia, Gaol Description and Entrance Books,1840
- NSW, Australia, Gaol Description and Entrance Books, Phoenix Hulk, July 1840
- "Committal of the Murderers of the Late Mr Noble." *The Sydney Morning Herald*, June 12, 1844
- "Supreme Criminal Court. Saturday, July 13. Murder." *Morning Chronicle*, July 17, 1844
- "Sydney." *Launceston Examiner*, August 3, 1844
- "Sydney News." *Southern Australian*, August 6, 1844
- "Sydney Intelligence." *The Courier*, September 7, 1844

- Laugesen, A. (2002) *Convict words, language in early colonial Australia.* Oxford University Press
- Karskens, G. (1984) *The Convict Road Station Site at Wisemans Ferry: an Historical and Archaeological Investigation.* Australian Historical Archaeology 2. https://ashadocs.org/aha/02/02_04_Karskens.pdf. Visited: June 14, 2018

Alexander Green
- NSW, Australia, Convict Indents, 1788 – 1842 (1824)
- Beckett, Ray & Beckett, Richard, 1936-1987 1980, *Hangman : the life and times of Alexander Green, public executioner to the colony of New South Wales*, Nelson, West Melbourne, Vic
- NSW, Australia, Colonial Secretary's Papers, 1788 – 1856 (1825)
- NSW, Australia Convict Ship Muster Rolls and Related Records, 1791 – 1849
- Australian Convict Transportation Registers – Other Fleet & Ships, 1791 – 1868 (1824)
- NSW, Australia, Colonial Secretary's Papers, 1788 – 1856 (1825)
- "Classified Advertising." *The Sydney Gazette and NSW Advertiser*, April 16, 1827
- "Advertising." *The Monitor*, June 21, 1827

- 1828 NSW, Australia Census
- NSW, Australia, Certificates of Freedom (1831)
- NSW, Australia, Gaol Description and Entrance Books, 1818 – 1930 (1833)
- NSW, Australia, Gaol Description and Entrance Books, 1818 – 1930 (January 1836)
- "Accidents, Offences & c." *The Sydney Herald*, April 11, 1836
- NSW, Australia, Gaol Description and Entrance Books, 1818 – 1930 (April 1836)
- "Police Incidents." *The Sydney Gazette and NSW Advertiser*, June 16, 1836
- "Family Notices." *The Sydney Gazette and NSW Advertiser*, June 24, 1837
- "Police Incidents." *The Sydney Gazette and NSW Advertiser*, June 24, 1837
- NSW, Australia, Registers of Convicts Applications to Marry, 1826 – 1851 (1838)
- "Court of Quarter." *Australasian Chronicle*, November 24, 1840
- "General Court of Quarter Sessions." *The Sydney Herald*, November 24, 1840
- "Quarter sessions." *The Australian*, November 26, 1840
- "Quarter Sessions." Monday, November 23. *The Colonist*, November 28, 1840

- NSW, Australia, Gaol Description and Entrance Books, 1818 – 1930 (1840)
- NSW, Australia, Gaol Description and Entrance Books, 1818 – 1930 (1840)
- NSW, Australia, Gaol Description and Entrance Books, 1818 – 1930 (1840)
- "Fatal Effects of the late Riot." *The Sydney Gazette and NSW Advertiser*, October 23, 1841
- "Supreme Court. Criminal Sittings – Thursday, October 21." *Australasian Chronical*, October 23, 1841
- "Police Court Business." *The Sydney Morning Herald*, October 12, 1843
- "Domestic Intelligence. Insolvency Proceedings. Monday." *The Sydney Morning Herald*, October 14, 1843
- "Domestic Intelligence. City Election." *The Sydney Morning Herald*, November 2, 1843
- "Sydney General Court of Quarter sessions." *The Sydney Morning Herald*, November 8, 1843
- NSW, Australia, Gaol Description and Entrance Books, 1818 – 1930 (1843)
- NSW, Australia, Gaol Description and Entrance Books, 1818 – 1930 (October 11, 1843)
- NSW, Australia, Criminal Court Records, 1830 – 1945 (November 4, 1843)

- NSW, Australia, Certificates of Freedom (1847)
- NSW, Australia, Gaol Description and Entrance Books, 1818 – 1930 (1849)
- NSW, Australia, Gaol Description and Entrance Books, 1818 – 1930 (July 1850)
- "Blood Lottery." *Bell's Life in Sydney and Sporting Reviewer*, August 6, 1853
- NSW, Australia, Gaol Description and Entrance Books, 1818 – 1930 (1853)
- NSW, Australia, Gaol Description and Entrance Books, 1818 – 1930 (July 1853)
- "Advertising." *The Sydney Morning Herald*, April 5, 1855
- NSW, Australia, Gaol Description and Entrance Books, 1818 – 1930 (1855)
- NSW, Australia, Gaol Description and Entrance Books, 1818 – 1930 (1855)
- NSW, Australia, Gaol Description and Entrance Books, 1818 – 1930 (1874)

Mary Morgan
- "Derby Races." *Derby Mercury*, August 13, 1789
- Australian Convict Transportation Registers – Second Fleet, 1787 - 1809
- Australia, List of Convicts with Particulars, 1788 – 1842 (1789)

- Australia, Convict Index 1788 - 1868
- NSW, Australia, Convict Indents, 1790 – 1791 Second Fleet
- NSW, Australia, Criminal Court Records, 1803
- NSW and Tasmania, Australia Convict Musters 1806
- NSW, Australia, Colonial Secretary's Paper, Aug 1809 (On list of all grants and leases of town allotments registered in the Colonial Secretary's Office)
- NSW, Australia, Land Grants, 8Aug 1809
- NSW and Tasmania, Australia Convict Musters, 1811
- "Classified Advertising." *The Sydney Gazette and NSW Advertiser*, May 2, 1812
- NSW, Australia, Colonial Secretary's Papers, 1814
- "Classified Advertising." *The Sydney Gazette and NSW Advertiser*, February 5, 1814
- NSW, Australia, Colonial Secretary's Papers, 1822
- NSW and Tasmania, Australia Convict Musters, 1822
- Australia, Marriage Index, 1822
- NSW, Australia, Colonial Secretary's Papers
- NSW and Tasmania, Australia Convict Musters, 1825

- NSW, Australia, Colonial Secretary's Papers, 25 August 1823
- "No. 1. To the Editor of "The Australian"." *The Australian*, February 14, 1827
- "Classified Advertising." *The Sydney Gazette and NSW Advertiser*, November 8, 1832
- NSW, Australia, Registers of Land Grants and Leases, 27 May 1834
- Australia, Death Index, 1835
- "Family Notices." *The Australian*, July 3, 1835
- "Tyranny." *The Sydney Gazette and NSW Advertiser*, July 4, 1835
- "Police Report." *The Sydney Gazette and NSW Advertiser*, July 7, 1835
- NSW, Australia, Registers of Coroners' Inquests, 1836
- Elizabeth Guilford, 'Morgan, Molly (1762-1835)', Australian Dictionary of Biography, National Centre of Biography, Australian National University, http://adb.anu.edu.au/biography/morgan-molly-2480/text3333. Published first in hardcopy 1967. Visited: April 24, 2018.
- Flynn, M. (2016). *Second Fleet*, Dictionary of Sydney http://dictionaryofsydney.org/entry/second_fleet. Visited: June 20, 2018.

- Needham, A & Riddler, L, Laurel, Hadley, Merle & Scott. (1992). *Women of the 1790 Neptune: the seventy-eight convicts named on the cover and those who came free*. Dural, NSW, A. Needham.

Israel Chapman
- *Old Bailey Proceedings Online* (www.oldbaileyonline.org, version 8.0, 01 May 2018), January 1818 (18180114).
- *Old Bailey Proceedings Online* (www.oldbaileyonline.org, version 8.0, 08 June 2018), January 1820 (18200112).
- NSW, Australia, Convict Indents
- Colonial Secretary's Paper's, May 19, 1820
- Colonial Secretary's Paper's, November 6, 1820
- NSW and Tasmania, Australia Convict Musters, 1822
- Government and General Orders. *The Sydney Gazette and NSW Advertiser* , January 18, 1822
- Colonial Secretary's Paper's, May 18, 1822
- "Classified Advertising." *The Sydney Gazette and NSW Advertiser*, June 7, 1822
- NSW and Tasmania, Australia Convict Musters, 1825
- "Quarter Sessions – Monday, Aug 29." *The Australian*, September 1, 1825

- "Classified Advertising." *The Sydney Gazette and NSW Advertiser*, December 7, 1827
- NSW, Australia, Returns of the Colony, 1828
- "(Domestic.)." *The Monitor,* April 12, 1828
- 1828 NSW, Australia Census
- NSW, Australia, Ticket of Leave, December 19, 1828
- "Shipping Intelligence." *The Sydney Gazette and NSW Advertiser,* February 10, 1829
- No title, *The Australian*, March 29, 1829
- "Shipping Intelligence. Arrivals." *The Sydney Gazette and NSW Advertiser*, March 31, 1829
- "Domestic Intelligence." *The Sydney Herald*, March 12, 1832
- *New South Wales, Australia, Unassisted Immigrant Passenger Lists, 1826-1922 (1833)*
- NSW, Australia, Gaol Description and Entrance Books, Sydney 1834 – 1838 (January 6, 1836)
- "Police Incidents." *The Sydney Herald*, January 30, 1834
- NSW, Australia, Gaol Description and Entrance Books January 6, 1837
- NSW, Australia, Gaol Description and Entrance Books Sydney 1837
- NSW Criminal Court Records, January 6, 1837

- NSW, Australia, Gaol Description and Entrance Books, 1841
- NSW, Australia, Gaol Description and Entrance Books, (June 23, 1842)
- NSW, Australia, Gaol Description and Entrance Books, Darlinghurst 1850 – 1855 (1852)
- Criminal Court Records, (May 28, 1852)
- Liverpool Asylum for the Infirm and Destitute. (March 2, 1863)
- Death Index, 1868
- Holland, E. (2012) *Outdoor Servants: The Stables.* Edwardian Promenade. www.edwardianpromenade.com/servants-2/outdoor-servants-the-stables/ Visited: June 13, 2018
- Bigge, J.T. (1823). *Report of the Commissioner of Inquiry on the Colony of New South Wales*, Adelaide: Library Board of South Australia, 1966.

Ann Yates

- *Old Bailey Proceedings Online* (www.oldbaileyonline.org, version 8.0, 01 May 2018), January 1796 (17960113).
- Australian Convict Transportation Registers – Second Fleet, 1789 - 1790

- NSW, Australia, Registers of Land Grants and Leases
- NSW, Australia, Convict Indents, 1797 – 1799
- NSW, Australia Convict Ship Muster Rolls and Related Records, 1798
- Australia, Marriage Index, 1798
- NSW and Tasmania, Australia Convict Musters, 1806
- "Classified Advertising." *The Sydney Gazette and NSW Advertiser*, November 5, 1809
- "Ship News." *The Sydney Gazette and NSW Advertiser*, March 10, 1810
- "Ship News." *The Sydney Gazette and NSW Advertiser*, March 31, 1810
- "Destruction of the Boyd." *The Sydney Gazette and NSW Advertiser*, April 21, 1810
- "Sydney." *The Sydney Gazette and NSW Advertiser*, May 23, 1812
- NSW, Australia, Colonial Secretary's Papers, 1813
- NSW and Tasmania, Australia Convict Musters, 1822
- NSW, Australia, Colonial Secretary's Papers, 1823
- NSW and Tasmania, Australia Convict Musters, 1825
- "The Boyd." *The Sydney Gazette and NSW Advertiser*, May 8, 1832

- "The Boyd Massacre." *The Kiama Independent, and Shoalhaven Advertiser*, December 3, 1895

Catherine Edwards
- Australian Convict Transportation Registers – Second Fleet
- NSW, Australia, Convict Indents, 1791
- "Fifty Convicts Attempt to walk to China from Parramatta in October, 1791." *Cumberland Argus and Fruitgrowers Advocate*, October 4, 1899 (1791)
- "Sydney." *The Sydney Gazette and NSW Advertiser*, December 8, 1805
- "Classified Advertising." *The Sydney Gazette and NSW Advertiser*, March 9, 1806
- "Bench of Magistrates. Saturday, March 15." *The Sydney Gazette and NSW Advertiser*, March 16, 1806
- "Bench of Magistrates. Saturday, April 5." *The Sydney Gazette and NSW Advertiser*, April 6, 1806
- NSW, Australia, Settler and Convict Lists, 1816
- "Criminal Court." *The Sydney Gazette and NSW Advertiser*, December 5, 1818

Ann Birmingham
- Australia, Convict Index, 1791

- Australian Convict Transportation Registers – Third Fleet
- Australia, Convict Index, 1796
- NSW and Tasmania, Australia Convict Musters, 1806
- "Sydney." *The Sydney Gazette and NSW Advertiser*, June 19, 1808
- Australia, Marriage Index 1820
- NSW, Australia, Colonial Secretary's Papers, (August 1822)
- NSW, Australia, Convict Indents, Annotated Printed Indentures, 1833
- NSW, Australia, Convict Indents, 1833
- NSW and Tasmania, Australia Convict Musters, 1825
- 1828 NSW Australia, Census
- "Rather Singular Case." *The Sydney Gazette and NSW Advertiser*, February 18, 1836
- "Domestic and Miscellaneous Intelligence." *The Australian*, February 19, 1836
- "Law Intelligence. Supreme Court – criminal side." *The Sydney Herald*, August 15, 1836
- "Supreme Court. Friday, August 12." *The Sydney Gazette and NSW Advertiser*, August 16, 1836
- "Supreme Court." *Commercial Journal and Advertiser*, August 17, 1836

- "Supreme Court. Friday, August 12th." *The Sydney Monitor*, August 17, 1836
- "Supreme Court. Thursday, November 3." *The Sydney Gazette and NSW Advertiser*, November 5, 1836
- "News of the Day." *The Sydney Monitor*, November 14, 1836
- NSW, Australia, Gaol Description and Entrance Books, 1837 - 1839
- NSW, Australia, Gaol Description and Entrance Books (January 25, 1838)
- NSW, Australia, Gaol Description and Entrance Books, (January 5, 1839)
- NSW, Australia, Gaol Description and Entrance Books, (April 15, 1839)
- Australia, Marriage Index, 1840
- 1841 NSW Australia, Census
- NSW, Australia, Gaol Description and Entrance Books (January 20, 1842)
- "Bathurst Circuit Court. Tuesday, March 29." *The Sydney Gazette and NSW Advertiser*, April 7, 1842
- "Bathurst Circuit Court. Thursday, March 3." *Sydney Free Press*, April 7, 1842
- "The Berrima and Mount Victoria Murderers." *The Sydney Gazette and NSW Advertiser*, May 3, 1842

- Office of Environment & Heritage, NSW Government. *Woodford Academy* www.environment.nsw.gov.au/heritageapp/ViewHeritageItemDetails.aspx?ID=5051258. Visited: June 14, 2018
- The Ghost at the Second Bridge – Poem by Henry Lawson, *PoemHunter*, https://www.poemhunter.com/poem/the-ghost-at-the-second-bridge/. Visited: June 4, 2019

Stephen Little
- NSW, Australia, Convict Indents, 1788 – 1842 (July 1, 1824)
- NSW, Australia, Colonial Secretary's Papers, 1788-1856 (December 27, 1824)
- NSW, Australia, Colonial Secretary's Papers, 1788-1856 (November 28, 1825)
- NSW, Australia, Colonial Secretary's Papers, 1788-1856 (12 December 1825)
- "The Police." *The Sydney Gazette and NSW Advertiser* , January 26, 1826
- "The Police." *The Sydney Gazette and NSW Advertiser* , March 1, 1826
- NSW, Australia, Gaol Description and Entrance Books, 1818-1930 (November 13, 1826) Sydney Gaol

- NSW, Australia, Certificates of Freedom, 1810-1814, 1827-1867 (January 31, 1831)
- NSW, Australia, Gaol Description and Entrance Books, 1818-1930 (February 22, 1831)
- "Court of Quarter Sessions." *The Sydney Herald*, May 2, 1831
- "Sydney Quarter Sessions." *The Sydney Gazette and NSW Advertiser* , April 28, 1831
- "Sydney Quarter Sessions." *The Sydney Gazette and NSW Advertiser* , April 30, 1831
- "Domestic Intelligence." *The Sydney Monitor* , April 27, 1831
- Bigge, J.T. (1823). *Report of the Commissioner of Inquiry on the Colony of New South Wales*, Adelaide: Library Board of South Australia, 1966.

Charles Anderson

- NSW, Australia, Convict Records, 1810-1891 Phoenix Hulk: Weekly Transportation Entrance Books, 1833 – 1837
- NSW, Australia, Convict Indents, 1788-1842
- NSW, Australia, Settler and Convict Lists, 1787-1834. (October 26, 1834)
- NSW, Australia, Convict Records, 1810-1891 (November 13, 1834)

- NSW, Australia, Criminal Court Records, 1830-1945 (March 16, 1835)
- NSW, Australia, Criminal Court Records, 1830-1945 (January 18, 1836)
- NSW, Australia, Criminal Court Records, 1830-1945 (August 12, 1836)
- NSW, Australia, Criminal Court Records, 1830-1945 (August 24, 1836)
- NSW, Australia, Criminal Court Records, 1830-1945 (August 30, 1836)
- NSW, Australia, Criminal Court Records, 1830-1945 (August 31, 1836)
- NSW, Australia, Gaol Description and Entrance Books, 1818-1930 Sydney Gaol (1837)
- NSW, Australia, Convict Records, 1810-1891 Port Macquarie: Monthly Returns (January 31, 1838)
- NSW, Australia, Convict Records, 1810-1891 Cockatoo Island: Index to Convicts, 1833-1834 (August 6, 1838)
- NSW, Australia, Convict Records, 1810-1891, Phoenix Hulk: Weekly Transportation Entrance Books, 1837-1840 (October 15, 1838)
- Vincent Barry, J. (1958). *Alexander Maconochie of Norfolk Island, A Study of a Pioneer in Penal Reform*, Melbourne, Oxford University Press.

- NSW, Australia, Hospital & Asylum Records, 1840-1913 Tarban Creek Lunatic Asylum (September 12, 1844)
- NSW, Australia, Tickets of Leave, 1810-1869 (May 24, 1853)
- NSW, Australia, Gaol Description and Entrance Books, 1818-1930 (January 5, 1854)

Mary Jackman
- NSW, Australia, Convict Indents, 1788-1842 (May 25, 1833)
- *Old Bailey Proceedings Online* (www.oldbaileyonline.org, version 8.0, 06 June 2018), June 1831 (18310630).
- NSW, Australia, Settler and Convict Lists, 1787-1834 Convicts arrived (May 25, 1833)
- NSW, Australia, Registers of Convicts' Applications to Marry, 1826-1851 (October 1, 1834)
- NSW, Australia, Tickets of Leave, 1810-1869 (September 9, 1841)
- "Government Gazette." *Australasian Chronicle*, September 25, 1841
- NSW, Australia, Registers of Convicts' Applications to Marry, 1826-1851
- NSW and Tasmania, Australia, Convict Pardons and Tickets of Leave, 1834-1859 Conditional Pardon (1849)

- "Government Gazette." *The Sydney Morning Herald*, June 9, 1849
- Hendriksen, G. Cowley, T. & Liston, C. (2008) *Women transported: life in Australia's convict female factories*, Parramatta, NSW, Parramatta City Council Heritage Centre.
- Liston, C. *Convict Women in the Female Factories of New South Wales*. Royal Australian Historical Society. http://www.rahs.org.au/wp-content/uploads/2015/08/Convict-Women-in-the-Female-Factories-of-New-South-Wales.pdf Visited: June 6, 2018.
- State Library of Queensland. (2018). *Thomas Balcombe*, Convict Records. https://convictrecords.com.au/convicts/balcombe/thomas/112567. Visited: June 16, 2018.

William Henshall
- NSW, Australia, Convict Indents, 1788-1842
- NSW, Australia, Settler and Convict Lists, 1787-1834
- NSW and Tasmania, Australia Convict Musters, 1806-1849 (1811)
- NSW, Australia, Convict Records, 1810-1891
- NSW, Australia, Certificates of Freedom, 1810-1814, 1827-1867 (September 12, 1812)

- NSW, Census and Population Books, 1811-1825 (1814)
- Australia, Marriage Index, 1788-1950
- NSW, Australia, Colonial Secretary's Papers, 1788-1856 (October 10, 1814)
- NSW, Australia, Colonial Secretary's Papers, 1788-1856, (May 14, 1817)
- NSW, Australia, Departing Crew and Passenger Lists, 1816-1825, 1898-1911, (December 15, 1817)
- NSW, Australia, Settler and Convict Lists, 1787-1834 (1821)
- *Holey Dollar*, National Museum Australia. http://www.nma.gov.au/collections/highlights/holey_dollar. Visited: May 23, 2018
- Lane, P & Fleig, P. *William Henshall: Maker of Holey Dollars and Dumps*, Journal of the Numismatic Association of Australia Inc. Volume 15

Robert Sidaway

- *Old Bailey Proceedings Online* (www.oldbaileyonline.org, version 8.0, 21 June 2018), September 1782 (17820911).
- *Old Bailey Proceedings Online* (www.oldbaileyonline.org, version 8.0, 21 June 2018), October 1782 (17821016).

- Australian Convict Transportation Registers – First Fleet, 1787-1788
- NSW, Australia, Convict Registers of Conditional and Absolute Pardons, 1788-1870 (November 29, 1792)
- Thorne, R. (1979). *Sydney's Lost Theatres: The First One Hundred Years, Parts One and Two.* Theatre Australia. http://www.rossthorne.com/downloads/SYDNEY_lost.PDF. Visited: June 22, 2018.
- Parsons, V. (Published first in hardcopy 1967). Sidaway, Robert (1758–1809), Australian Dictionary of Biography, National Centre of Biography, Australian National University, http://adb.anu.edu.au/biography/sidaway-robert-2660/text3681. Visited: June 22, 2018.
- NSW, Australia, Colonial Secretary's Papers, 1788-1856 (November 6, 1794)
- NSW, Australia, Registers of Land Grants and Leases, 1792-1867 (January 16, 1796)
- NSW, Australia, Land Grants, 1788-1963 (December 1804)
- "Ship News." *The Sydney Gazette and NSW Advertiser*, October 27, 1805
- "Sydney." *The Sydney Gazette and NSW Advertiser*, November 3, 1805

- NSW, Australia, Colonial Secretary's Papers, 1788-1856 (January 1, 1806)
- "General Orders." *The Sydney Gazette and NSW Advertiser*, April 13, 1806
- NSW and Tasmania, Australia Convict Musters, 1806-1849 (1806)
- NSW, Australia, Colonial Secretary's Papers, 1788-1856 (July 1806)
- "Family Notices." *The Sydney Gazette and NSW Advertiser*, October 5, 1806
- NSW, Australia, Colonial Secretary's Papers, 1788-1856 (April 1809)
- NSW, Australia, Colonial Secretary's Papers, 1788-1856 (January 15, 1810)

Ann Jarvis
- Australian Convict Transportation Registers – Other Fleets & Ships, 1791-1868 (June 8, 1828)
- NSW, Australia, Convict Indents, 1788-1842 (1828)
- NSW, Australia, Gaol Description and Entrance Books, 1818-1930 Sydney Gaol (December 10, 1828)
- NSW, Australia, Land Grants, 1788-1963 (February 7, 1831)
- "Classified Advertising." *The Sydney Gazette and NSW Advertiser*, April 21, 1831

- "Classified Advertising." *The Sydney Gazette and NSW Advertiser*, April 28, 1831
- "Classified Advertising." *The Sydney Gazette and NSW Advertiser*, May 5, 1831
- "Classified Advertising." *The Sydney Gazette and NSW Advertiser*, December 20, 1832
- NSW, Australia, Gaol Description and Entrance Books, 1818-1930, (January 30, 1833)
- NSW, Australia, Certificates of Freedom, 1810-1814, 1827-1867 (April 28, 1834)
- "Classified Advertising." *The Sydney Gazette and NSW Advertiser*, August 30, 1834
- NSW, Australia, Certificates of Freedom, 1810-1814, 1827-1867 (July 15, 1835)
- NSW, Australia, Criminal Court Records, 1830-1945 (March 15, 1852)
- New South Wales, Australia, Criminal Court Records, 1830-1945 (May 13, 1852)
- Daniels, K. (1998). *Convict Women*, St Leonards, NSW, Allen & Unwin.

William Cluer
- Piece 1, series HO26, Home Office:Criminal Registers, Middlesex, 1791 – 1849, class 26, findmypast
- Australian Convict Transportation Registers – Other Fleets & Ships, 1791-1868

- NSW, Australia, Settler and Convict Lists, 1787-1834 (1804)
- "Classified Advertising." *The Sydney Gazette and NSW Advertiser*, December 23, 1804
- "Classified Advertising." *The Sydney Gazette and NSW Advertiser*, December 30, 1804
- "Classified Advertising." *The Sydney Gazette and NSW Advertiser*, August 17, 1806
- NSW and Tasmania, Australia Convict Musters, 1806-1849 (1806)
- "Classified Advertising." *The Sydney Gazette and NSW Advertiser*, May 15, 1808
- Australia, Marriage Index, 1788-1950 (1809)
- *The Sydney Gazette and NSW Advertiser* , June 11, 1809
- "Classified Advertising." *The Sydney Gazette and NSW Advertiser*, July 30, 1809
- NSW, Australia, Colonial Secretary's Papers, 1788-1856 (April 15, 1812)
- NSW, Australia, Convict Registers of Conditional and Absolute Pardons, 1788-1870
- NSW, Australia, Colonial Secretary's Papers, 1788-1856 (January 1813)
- NSW, Australia, Convict Registers of Conditional and Absolute Pardons, 1788-1870
- "Classified Advertising." *The Sydney Gazette and NSW Advertiser*, February 27, 1813

- NSW, Australia, Colonial Secretary's Papers, 1788-1856
- NSW, Census and Population Books, 1811-1825 (1814)
- "Classified Advertising." *The Sydney Gazette and NSW Advertiser*, January 27, 1816
- "Classified Advertising." *The Sydney Gazette and NSW Advertiser*, June 20, 1818
- "Classified Advertising." *The Sydney Gazette and NSW Advertiser*, July 18, 1818
- "Classified Advertising." *The Sydney Gazette and NSW Advertiser*, September 19, 1818
- "Classified Advertising." *The Sydney Gazette and NSW Advertiser*, May 8, 1819
- "Classified Advertising." *The Sydney Gazette and NSW Advertiser*, November 27, 1819
- "Classified Advertising." *The Sydney Gazette and NSW Advertiser*, April 21, 1821
- "Classified Advertising." *The Sydney Gazette and NSW Advertiser*, April 28, 1821
- "Hobart Town." *Hobart town Gazette and Van Dieman's Land Advertiser (Tas.: 1821 – 1825)*, December 7, 1822
- NSW and Tasmania, Australia Convict Musters, 1806-1849 (1822)
- "Classified Advertising." *The Sydney Gazette and NSW Advertiser*, January 30, 1823

- NSW, Australia, Registers of Land Grants and Leases, 1792-1867 (June 30, 1823)
- NSW, Australia, Departing Crew and Passenger Lists, 1816-1825, 1898-1911 (June 8, 1824)
- Australia, Death Index, 1787-1985 (1824)
- NSW and Tasmania, Australia Convict Musters, 1806-1849 (1825)
- NSW, Australia Census 1828
- NSW, Australia, Land Grants, 1788-1963 (August 5, 1829)
- NSW, Australia, Land Grants, 1788-1963 (January 15, 1838)
- NSW, Australia, Land Grants, 1788-1963 (November 16, 1839)
- GoJak, D. & Stuart, I. (1999). The Potential for the Archaeological Study of Clay Tobacco Pipes from Australian Sites, Australasian Historical Archaeology, 17. http://www.asha.org.au/pdf/australasian_historical_archaeology/17_04_Gojak.pdf.Visited: June 24, 2018.

Samuel Wheeler
- Australian Convict Transportation Registers – First Fleet, 1787-1788
- Australia, Convict Index, 1788-1868

- NSW, Australia, Settler and Convict Lists, 1787-1834
- NSW, Australia, Convict Records, 1810-1891
- NSW, Australia, Colonial Secretary's Papers, 1788-1856 (February 20, 1794)
- NSW, Australia, Colonial Secretary's Papers, 1788-1856 (April 10, 1802)
- NSW, Australia, Colonial Secretary's Papers, 1788-1856 (June 12, 1811)
- NSW, Australia, Land Records, 1811-1870 (June 14, 1811)
- NSW, Australia Census 1828
- NSW and Tasmania, Australia Convict Musters, 1806-1849 (1825)
- McLaren, A. (2013) *Convict Geographies of Early Colonial Sydney*. https://ses.library.usyd.edu.au/bitstream/2123/10243/1/McLaren,%20A_Thesis_2013.docx.pdf. Visited: June 15, 2018
- Bonomo, R. (2013). *Convict Brick Mould, History*. Australian National Maritime Museum. http://collections.anmm.gov.au/objects/143568. Visited: June 15, 2018
- Stocks, R. (2008). *New evidence for local manufacture of artefacts at Parramatta 1790 – 1830*, Australasian Historical Archaeology, 26.

http://www.asha.org.au/pdf/australasian_historical_archaeology/26_04_Stocks.pdf.
Visited: June 15, 2018

Abraham Lawley
- England & Wales, Criminal Registers, 1791-1892 (1824)
- England & Wales, Criminal Registers, 1791-1892 (1828)
- NSW, Australia, Convict Indents, 1788-1842 (November 9, 1829)
- Nason, J. (2009/2010) *A little piece of my heart...The Convict Love Token collection of the National Museum of Australia.* Journal of the Numismatic Association of Australia, Volume 20 www.numismatics.org.au/pdfjournal/Vol20/Vol%2020%20Article%203.pdf. Visited: June 23, 2018.
- NSW, Australia, Gaol Description and Entrance Books, 1818-1930 (1833)
- NSW, Australia, Convict Records, 1810-1891 (September 5, 1833)
- NSW and Tasmania, Australia, Convict Pardons and Tickets of Leave, 1834-1859 1834-1838
- NSW, Australia, Convict Savings Bank Books, 1824-1886

- 1841 New South Wales, Australia, Census
- NSW, Australia, Certificates of Freedom, 1810-1814, 1827-1867 (October 20, 1843)
- NSW, Australia, Criminal Court Records, 1830-1945 (June 28, 1844)
- NSW, Australia, Criminal Court Records, 1830-1945 (August 30, 1844)
- "Law Intelligence." *The Sydney Morning Herald*, June 5, 1848
- "Central Criminal Court." *The Maitland Mercury and Hunter River General Advertiser*, June 7, 1848
- "Interior. Terrible Flood and Loss of Life at Goulburn." *Empire*, July 2, 1852
- "Police Reports." *The Goulburn Herald and County of Argyle Advertiser*, June 30, 1855
- "Domestic Intelligence." *The Goulburn Herald and County of Argyle Advertiser*, December 1, 1855
- New South Wales, Australia, Certificates for Publicans' Licences, 1830-1849, 1853-1899 (December 4, 1855)
- "Insolvency Proceedings." *The Maitland Mercury and Hunter River General Advertiser*, April 7, 1860
- "Monthly Commercial Review." *The Sydney Morning Herald*, April 14, 1860

- "Country Districts." *Freemans Journal*, May 7, 1862
- NSW, Australia, Gaol Description and Entrance Books, 1818-1930 (March 24, 1866) Darlinghurst Gaol
- NSW, Australia, Criminal Court Records, 1830-1945 (May 9, 1870)
- NSW, Australia, Criminal Court Records, 1830-1945 (July 26, 1871)
- NSW, Australia, Criminal Court Records, 1830-1945 (April 4, 1876)
- NSW, Australia, Criminal Court Records, 1830-1945 (March 24, 1866) Braidwood

Ann Moran
- NSW, Australia, Convict Indents, 1788-1842 (June 26, 1802)
- NSW and Tasmania, Australia Convict Musters, 1806-1849 (1806)
- NSW, Census and Population Books, 1811-1825 (1814)
- Australia, Marriage Index, 1788-1950 (1814)
- NSW and Tasmania, Australia Convict Musters, 1806-1849 (1825)
- Timbury, C. (2013). *First Fleet Cattle*, First Fleet Fellowship Victoria Inc. https://firstfleetfellowship.org.au/library/first-fleet-cattle/. Visited: June 16, 2018

John Lane
- NSW, Australia, Convict Indents, 1788-1842 (1831)
- "General Quarter Sessions, Conjugal Affection," *The Sydney Monitor*, August 10, 1831
- "Domestic Intelligence," *The Sydney Herald*, August 8, 1831
- NSW and Tasmania, Australia Convict Musters, 1806-1849 (1837)
- NSW and Tasmania, Australia, Convict Pardons and Tickets of Leave, 1834-1859 (1835)
- NSW, Australia, Tickets of Leave, 1810-1869 (October 7, 1839)
- NSW, Australia, Gaol Description and Entrance Books, 1818-1930 (September 10, 1840)
- NSW, Australia, Tickets of Leave, 1810-1869 (December 5, 1840)
- NSW, Australia, Tickets of Leave, 1810-1869 (May 4, 1842)
- NSW, Australia, Convict Registers of Conditional and Absolute Pardons, 1788-1870 (February 1, 1845)
- NSW and Tasmania, Australia, Convict Pardons and Tickets of Leave, 1834-1859 (1848)

- Prima, M. (2005). *History of the Umbrella*, Literary Liaisons. http://www.literary-liaisons.com/article056.htm. Visited: June 17, 2018.

William Lock Thurston
- *Old Bailey Proceedings Online* (www.oldbaileyonline.org, version 8.0, 04 June 2018), April 1809, trial of EZEKIEL LOCKLEADER , alias LOCKTHURSTON ROBERT LOCKLEADER , alias LOCKTHURSTON (t18090412-45).
- Australia, Convict Index, 1788-1868 (1810)
- NSW and Tasmania, Australia Convict Musters, 1806-1849 (1811)
- NSW, Australia, Convict Registers of Conditional and Absolute Pardons, 1788-1870 (January 31, 1814)
- NSW, Australia, Colonial Secretary's Papers, 1788-1856
- NSW, Census and Population Books, 1811-1825 (1819)
- NSW and Tasmania, Australia Convict Musters, 1806-1849 (1822)
- NSW, Census and Population Books, 1811-1825 (1822)
- NSW and Tasmania, Australia Convict Musters, 1806-1849 (1825)

- "List of Licensed Victuallers for Sydney." *The Australian*, March 7, 1828
- 1828 New South Wales, Australia, Census
- NSW, Australia, Colonial Secretary's Papers, 1788-1856 (October 28, 1825)
- NSW, Australia, Certificates for Publicans' Licences, 1830-1849, 1853-1899 (1831)
- "Licensed Publicans of Sydney." *The Australian,* August 5, 1831
- "Advance Australia." *The Sydney Gazette and NSW Advertiser*, January 5, 1832
- "Domestic Intelligence." *The Sydney Herald*, January 9, 1832
- The New South Wales Calendar and General Post Office Directory, 1832
- 1841 NSW, Australia, Census
- Roberts, M. (2015) *The Rock's Infamous Black Dog*, Time Gents, Australian Pub Project. https://timegents.com/2015/04/04/the-rocks-infamous-black-dog/. Visited: July 1, 2018.
- *Norfolk Chronicle*, March 11, 1809. British Newspaper Archive. www.britishnewspaperarchive.co.uk. Visited: July 1, 2018
- *Norfolk Chronicle*, March 25, 1809. British Newspaper Archive.

- www.britishnewspaperarchive.co.uk. Visited: July 1, 2018
- *166787 Thurston,* Free Settler or Felon, Jen Willetts. https://www.jenwilletts.com/searchaction.php?page=1&surname=thurston&ship=&firstname=daniel. Visited: July 1, 2018.

John McEntire
- Series: HO47, Judges Reports on criminals 1784 – 1830 Correpsondance, 1784 – 1785, Piece number: 3
- Australia, Convict Index, 1788-1868 (1788 Alexander)
- Australian Convict Transportation Registers – First Fleet, 1787-1788
- NSW, Australia, Settler and Convict Lists, 1787-1834
- Australia, Death Index, 1787-1985
- Karskens, G. (2009). *The Colony: a history of early Sydney*, Allen & Unwin.
- Vincent Smith, K. (2010). *Pemulwuy*, Dictionary of Sydney, http://dictionaryofsydney.org/entry/pemulwuy. Viewed: June, 18 2018
- Worgan, G, B. (1757 – 1838). *Journal of a first fleet surgeon*, Library Council of New South Wales; Library of Australian History.

- Tench, W. (1758/9 – 1833). Edited and introduced by: Flannery, T, F. (1956). *1788: Comprising a narrative of the expedition to Botany Bay and A complete account of the settlement at Port Jackson*, Melbourne, Text Publishing.

Francis Ambrose
- *Old Bailey Proceedings Online* (www.oldbaileyonline.org, version 8.0, 27 March 2019), December 1827, trial of FRANCIS AMBROSE (t18271206-122).
- NSW, Australia, Convict Indents, 1788-1842
- *Wilets, J. Convict Ship Bussorah Merchant 1828*. Free Settler or Felon, https://www.jenwilletts.com/convict_ship_bussorah_merchant_1828.htm. Visited: June 4, 2019
- Bateson, Charles & Library of Australian History (1983). *The Convict Ships, 1787-1868* (Australian ed). Library of Australian History, Sydney
- NSW, Australia, Gaol Description and Entrance Books, 1818-1930 (July 4, 1829)
- New South Wales, Australia, Gaol Description and Entrance Books, 1818-1930 (April 22, 1833)

- "Classified Advertising." *The Sydney Gazette and NSW Advertiser*, April 25, 1833
- "Classified Advertising." *The Sydney Gazette and NSW Advertiser*, August 15, 1833
- New South Wales, Australia, Gaol Description and Entrance Books, 1818-1930 (September 3, 1833)
- New South Wales, Australia, Gaol Description and Entrance Books, 1818-1930 (January 1836)
- New South Wales, Australia, Criminal Court Records, 1830-1945 (February 22, 1836)
- New South Wales, Australia, Criminal Court Records, 1830-1945 (April 29, 1836)
- New South Wales, Australia, Gaol Description and Entrance Books, 1818-1930 (May 6, 1836
- New South Wales, Australia, Criminal Court Records, 1830-1945 (November 1, 1836)
- New South Wales, Australia, Gaol Description and Entrance Books, 1818-1930 (September 28, 1837)

Catherine Harvey
- London, England, Church of England Marriages and Banns, 1754-1921 (1793)

- *Old Bailey Proceedings Online* (www.oldbaileyonline.org, version 8.0, 17 April 2019), November 1803 (18031130).
- *Old Bailey Proceedings Online (www.oldbaileyonline.org, version 8.0, 17 April 2019), September 1811, trial of CATHERINE GODDARD (t18110918-147).*
- "Sundays Post." *Bury and Norwich Post*, December 11, 1811
- New South Wales, Australia, Convict Indents, 1788-1842 (1812)
- New South Wales, Australia, Certificates of Freedom, 1810-1814, 1827-1867 (July 5, 1813)
- New South Wales, Australia, Colonial Secretary's Papers, 1788-1856 (July 24, 1813)
- New South Wales, Australia, Colonial Secretary's Papers, 1788-1856 (July 1820)
- New South Wales and Tasmania, Australia Convict Musters, 1806-1849 (1822)
- New South Wales, Australia, Colonial Secretary's Papers, 1788-1856 (1822)
- 1828 New South Wales, Australia Census (Australian Copy)
- New South Wales and Tasmania, Australia Convict Musters, 1806-1849 (1837)
- New South Wales, Australia, Convict Records, 1810-1891 (October 21, 1840)
- Australia, Death Index, 1787-1985 (1840)

Frederick Brook Carrick
- Gloucestershire, England, Church of England Marriages and Banns, 1754-1938 (September 5, 1814)
- Oxfordshire, England, Church of England Births and Baptisms, 1813-1915 (November 28, 1814)
- Oxfordshire, England, Church of England Births and Baptisms, 1813-1915 (30 June 1816)
- Oxfordshire, England, Church of England Deaths and Burials, 1813-1965 (November 12, 1817)
- *Old Bailey Proceedings Online* (www.oldbaileyonline.org, version 8.0, 21 May 2019), September 1817, trial of FREDERICK CARRICK (t18170917-164).
- *Old Bailey Proceedings Online* (www.oldbaileyonline.org, version 8.0, 09 April 2019), December 1817 (18171203).
- New South Wales, Australia, Convict Indents, 1788-1842 (September 14, 1818)
- New South Wales and Tasmania, Australia Convict Musters, 1806-1849 (1825)
- 1828 New South Wales, Australia Census (TNA Copy)
- Australia, Births and Baptisms, 1792-1981 (April 1, 1826)

- Australia, Births and Baptisms, 1792-1981 (June 3, 1827)
- Australia, Death Index, 1787-1985 (1828)
- New South Wales, Australia, Tickets of Leave, 1810-1869 (July 9, 1831)
- New South Wales, Australia, Certificates for Publicans' Licences, 1830-1849, 1853-1899 (July 11, 1835)
- "Family Notices." *The Sydney Times*, November 7, 1834
- *New South Wales, Australia, Land Grants, 1788-1963 (November 18, 1836)*
- "Advertising." *The Colonist*, December 1, 1836
- "Colonial Secretary's Office. Sydney, 16th May, 1837 PARDONS." *The Sydney Gazette and NSW Advertiser*, May 20, 1837
- "Advertising." *Commercial Journal and Advertiser*, October 30, 1839
- New South Wales, Australia, Certificates for Publicans' Licences, 1830-1849, 1853-1899 (June 29, 1840)
- "Supreme Court." *Australasian Chronicle*, June 3, 1841
- "Law Intelligence, Supreme Court,-Tuesday, 1st June." *The Sydney Herald*, June 3, 1841
- "WEDNESDAY, 2ND JUNE." *The Sydney Herald*, June 3, 1841

- Sydney, Australia, Cemetery Headstone Transcriptions, 1837 – 2003 (1844)

Isaac Crane
- *Old Bailey Proceedings Online* (www.oldbaileyonline.org, version 8.0, 11 May 2019), February 1812, trial of THOMAS DUTTON ISAAC CRANE (t18120219-79).
- *Old Bailey Proceedings Online* (www.oldbaileyonline.org, version 8.0, 11 May 2019), September 1812, trial of ISAAC CRANE (t18120916-110).
- UK, Prison Hulk Registers and Letter Books, 1802-1849 (May 26, 1813)
- Bateson, Charles & Library of Australian History (1983). *The Convict Ships, 1787-1868* (Australian ed). Library of Australian History, Sydney
- New South Wales, Australia, Convict Indents, 1788-1842 (1814)
- New South Wales, Census and Population Books, 1811-1825 (1814)
- England & Wales, Criminal Registers, 1791-1892 (1820)
- Australia, Marriage Index, 1788-1950 (1822)
- Australia, Births and Baptisms, 1792-1981 (March 27, 1823)

- Australia, Births and Baptisms, 1792-1981 (January 31, 1825)
- New South Wales, Australia, Tickets of Leave, 1810-1869 (July 20, 1832)
- Australia, Marriage Index, 1788-1950 *(1839)*
- "News from the Interior. (From our various corresondents.) Cambelltown." *The Sydney Morning Herald*, March 4, 1843.
- "Windsor." *The Sydney Morning Herald*, August 1, 1855.

Acknowledgements

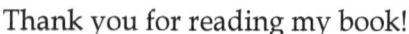

Thank you for reading my book!

If you enjoyed the book please leave a review on Amazon letting me know your thoughts. I would be delighted to hear from any descendants of the convicts within this publication.

I would also like to say thank you to my family and friends for their support and encouragement. Thank you to the teams at Lynk Manuscript Assessment Service and Happy Self Publishing for all of their work. Lastly, I would like to say a special thank you to Tracey Wearne and my son Oliver Twemlow.

Jennifer Twemlow

www.ingramcontent.com/pod-product-compliance
Lightning Source LLC
Chambersburg PA
CBHW020318010526
44107CB00054B/1890